# wabisugi | the art of resilience for everyday warriors

By Jenny Sutton and Graham Wilson

ISBN 978-0-9931390-2-4

**Published by Successfactory, Chester, United Kingdom**
**For more copies of this book, please email: info@thesuccessfactory.co.uk**
**Tel: +44 (0) 1829 771770**

Illustrations by Martin Teviotdale
Edited by Anne Wilson

# Wabi-Sabi

"a way of living that focuses on finding beauty within the imperfections of life and accepting peacefully the natural cycle of growth and decay"

# Kintsugi

"the art of precious scars"

# Wabisugi

"the art of resilience for everyday warriors"

## Meet the Authors

### A personal message from Jenny and Graham

### Welcome to **wabi**sugi

You're probably wondering what the word wabisugi means.

We will define it more fully later in the book. But for now, it is a word that we created to outline our resilience approach combining two Japanese philosophies, wabi-sabi and kintsugi!

It's your guide to becoming more resilient. We are defining resilience as the capacity to recover quickly from difficulties, your mental toughness.

The book is a story of resilience plus a framework to help you work out what you need to become even more resilient, and more importantly, the tools to develop your mental toughness.

During our work, we meet many people who are struggling in today's fast-paced world. Many feel overwhelmed, stressed and not enjoying life to the full.

This book is our attempt to share our learning about teaching resiliency as part of our leadership programmes over the past 27 years.

It identifies a tried, tested and proven framework and provides the tools you require to be the best you can be.

We tell Jenny's story to help you understand the mindset and learning required to become mentally tough. It is not a story of Olympic champions, elite special forces or superhuman beings, just a normal young girl overcoming the personal challenges in life.

Wabisugi is a book full of practical insights for everyday people to use in their lives.

We hope you enjoy it.

Every success,
**Jenny and Graham**

"WHETHER YOU BELIEVE YOU CAN, OR BELIEVE YOU CAN'T, YOU ARE ABSOLUTELY RIGHT"

HENRY FORD

# CONTENTS

## SECTION 1

## SECTION 2

## SECTION 3

## SECTION 4

## SECTION 5

# WELCOME TO YOUR

## TOTAL Resiliency TOOLKIT

**WARNING,**
this book could
**RADICALLY CHANGE**
your **RESULTS!**

"THE HUMAN CAPACITY FOR BURDEN IS LIKE BAMBOO – FAR MORE FLEXIBLE THAN YOU'D EVER BELIEVE AT FIRST GLANCE."

JODI PICOULT, MY SISTER'S KEEPER

# Who is this book for?

Wabisugi is for everyday warriors, game changers and leaders who want to thrive in today's world.

It's for people who want to deliver in mission-critical situations, even when the going gets tough.

It's for people who feel overwhelmed, stressed and unhappy with their lives and who are searching for a new way of doing things. It's for those ready to take back control and live their best life possible.

Sooner or later, we all have to cope with setbacks and failures. What sets successful people apart is their ability to demonstrate resilience in the face of these challenges and adversity. It's about how they bounce back and keep going.

Resilient people are more confident, agile, and adaptable. They can navigate change without fear when problems occur. Delve into the world of wabisugi, and you will discover a collection of tried and tested tips and hints that will support your journey.

Mastering the art of wabisugi enables you to have more energy, be calmer, less stressed, and feel in control. Find more joy, develop a growth mindset, be always open to learning and most important of all, put that smile back on your face!

**Does this sound appealing?**
**Then let's jump right in and get started.**

# How to get the most out of your wabisugi journey

**Before we begin, it is useful to understand the flow and journey we are going on together.**

## Your wabisugi journey

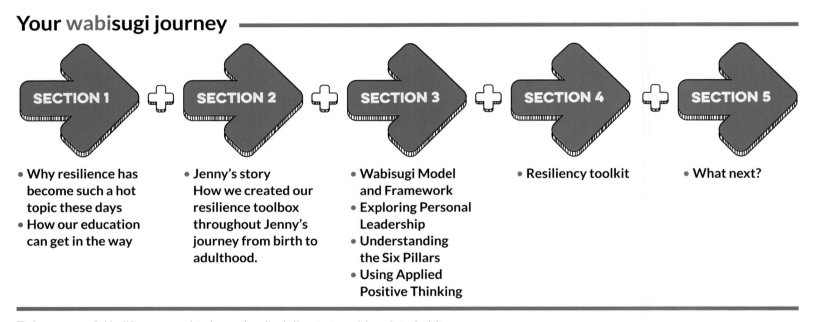

**SECTION 1**
- Why resilience has become such a hot topic these days
- How our education can get in the way

**SECTION 2**
- Jenny's story How we created our resilience toolbox throughout Jenny's journey from birth to adulthood.

**SECTION 3**
- Wabisugi Model and Framework
- Exploring Personal Leadership
- Understanding the Six Pillars
- Using Applied Positive Thinking

**SECTION 4**
- Resiliency toolkit

**SECTION 5**
- What next?

To be successful in life, we need to have the discipline to turn ideas into habits.

This book will share the fundamental philosophy that underpins resilience which is at the heart of your wabisugi journey.

We will also share the tools to help you create positive ways of working and performance habits.

## Why has resilience become such a hot topic these days?

I'm sure you'll agree that we live in a challenging world of fast change!

Our disruptive, volatile, uncertain, ambiguous and complex world is causing plenty of challenge, resulting in many people feeling stressed and overwhelmed.

A world where many people are asking, "What on earth happened!"

What used to work previously doesn't seem to work in the same way in today's world. It's like someone has changed the rules for our success.

We can't just rely on our experiences to deliver extraordinary results anymore. Something has happened. The pace of change is so fast we are struggling to keep up.

It's even harder now to achieve the results we are looking for. We tend to put more pressure on ourselves and work even harder to try and achieve better results. We get trapped on the 'hamster wheel' doing the same things but faster!

In today's tough world, we need to look at new ways of leading. One of those new ways is to develop our resiliency skills.

Let's explore what we've discovered about resiliency and how we can all start **delivering extraordinary results.**

# Social expectations can get in the way!

First of all, we need to explore the 'Beauty of Imperfection.'

When it comes to what things should look like, it's easy to get caught up in the false mindset of being perfect.

The notion of symmetry, ideal proportions shaped by universal laws, mathematics and the search for perfection are, in fact, flawed. You only have to look at nature to see that.

In today's social media frenzy, it is easy to compare with others and feel that you are not perfect, causing untold damage to our well-being and particularly that of our children.

It hasn't always been that way. Take the Baroque period, for example, a period defined by its art and architecture's grandeur and luxury. However, its name came from the word barroco, a Portuguese term for an irregularly-shaped pearl!

Before that, we had the Japanese culture of wabi-sabi. A philosophy focused on accepting transience and imperfection; beauty is imperfect, impermanent, and incomplete. Wabi-sabi supports the 'magnificence of imperfection'.

Kintsugi is the Japanese art of repairing broken pottery by mending the damaged areas with powdered gold, silver, or platinum. It treats breakage and repair as part of an object's history rather than something to disguise.

Wabisugi is a new word we created to combine the philosophy of wabi-sabi and the practice of kintsugi.

Wabisugi is the art of resilience for the everyday warrior.

## How our education can get in the way!

One of the key elements that we will explore in this book is the importance of support to enable you to be more resilient. It doesn't help that in school, we were taught that teamworking and collaboration is cheating!

We shall explain. If we go back to your classroom and your teacher asks you a question. What would be your behaviour? You'd probably think about the question, and if you knew the answer, you would put your hand up. The teacher would then tell you if you were right or wrong.

What would have happened if you started to collaborate and have conversations with your classmates when the teacher asked you the question? We're sure they would have told you off and asked you to be quiet!

These early years taught us that collaboration is cheating, and we should come up with all the answers ourselves.

We take this belief-system into adulthood, putting so much pressure on ourselves, and spend so much energy trying to work out all the answers to our problems, challenges and opportunities using this mindset. We need to change that and start to use the power of teams and support.

## Do you remember getting your school report?

For most of us there was probably one subject we didn't like much because the teacher didn't inspire us or ignite our passion around the subject.

Imagine getting your school report, and in every other subject apart from the one you hate, you get top marks. You don't care about the one poor result as you don't like the subject, so you go home feeling proud of a good year and excited to show your parents the report.

You arrive home, and you lay your school report on the dining room table to share. What would be the first thing they would say? Let me guess - I bet they said, "What happened there then?" Pointing out the one poor result, ignoring all the fantastic results you achieved in the other subjects.

Am I right?

So how does this play out in our lives?

We try to strive for perfection in everything rather than focusing on our strengths. We put so much wasted energy and effort into developing areas we will never be good at, impacting your confidence and resiliency. What mindsets have you developed, subconsciously, that could be getting in your way of being more resilient?

# Jenny's Story

## We were so excited.

It was the 24th of May, 1997 and we were celebrating our daughter Joanne's 4th birthday with a party at home. One of the activities we had arranged was a Punch and Judy show. It was so much fun, and Joanne and her friends enjoyed it so much. Little did we know that the fun and frolics were to act as the catalyst for Jenny's early arrival the very next day!

Jennifer Anne Wilson was born early in the morning on 25th May.

It was a challenging birth.

The excitement of the imminent arrival of our baby soon turned to fear and pain. I felt helpless, just watching, unsure of what was happening, and only being there for support was very difficult for me. I'm a fixer, not a watcher!

Due to various circumstances and situations during gestation and birth, Jenny was born not breathing, resulting in oxygen starvation. The first few days were challenging as Jenny began fitting, which caused her to stop breathing, and I remember the constant sound of the alarms going off whilst Jenny was resuscitated time and time again. As a parent, all you want is to take your child's pain away and will her to survive.

The nursing team were amazing and allowed us to support Jenny in every way we could. They were genuinely skilled in adapting to the situation and using their experience and knowledge to create solutions. It took hours of kangaroo hugs, cuddles and positivity to get through this time. Not knowing what was wrong was hard as the future was unknown. We were in the fog! The only vision we had was survival.

> ## "IF YOUR HEART IS BROKEN, MAKE ART WITH THE PIECES."
> ### SHANE KOYCZAN

Seeing your baby plugged into various machines, being fed by a drip, and pumped full of drugs to keep her alive was very hard. I just remember feeling a deep sense of love and determination setting in, even though I was unaware of what was wrong and if she would survive. One of the key learnings I took from this time was that you don't want sugar-coated conversations; you need truth. With the truth, you can move forward. Your well-being is preserved, not diminished when you can see the reality of the situation and respond to it. When the facts are unknown or not shared, you are left in the wilderness, helpless and frightened.

As the days passed, we rejoiced at each little improvement no matter how small, and it was a good day when Jenny could begin Nasogastric tube feeding. We had to learn how to feed a small soft tube up Jenny's nose, down the back of her throat, making sure it went down the oesophagus and into her tiny stomach, and it was terrifying at first. Jenny's Mum was able to express her breast milk to ensure Jenny received all the vital nutrients essential for her survival, and we soon became experts at feeding Jenny this way.

With a challenging leadership training business to run and a 4-year-old daughter at home, the situation became a huge challenge to overcome. Added to the fact that Jenny's Mum broke her ankle, and her Dad was dying from an aggressive form of cancer made it so tough.

We kept our resolve as I believed the key to resilience was not to accept the situation but to strive for a way through, and with family and friends' support, we did just that and managed to survive those early and uncertain days.

After several weeks of being supported by the fantastic special care team, I will never forget the first day Jenny smiled, my heart sang, and shortly after, we were finally able to take Jenny home – what a special day that was. Our little fighter had survived!

# The Early Years

**We promised ourselves to bring up our children to be caring, kind, courageous and confident. We focused on the importance of creating experiences and memories rather than just material possessions and toys.**

It is easy to focus too much on one child and forget the other, but Joanne, Jenny's sister, enjoyed being a big sister and understood that Jenny needed extra care and took everything in her stride, hoping that her sister would be ok. It is, however, easy to forget the challenges a sibling faces when their sister is disabled. Trying to keep life as normal as possible for Joanne became a priority.

It soon became apparent that our real challenges had only just begun. It took several months before we could get a proper diagnosis and start to look at what the future would hold for Jenny and us as a family.

It's easy during these moments of high emotion to fall into the trap of the blame game. Whose fault was it? Who can we pin this on? In reality, feeling like this is useless and sends you into a victim mentality. We had to be strong for Jenny and Joanne and focus on what we could control, not what we couldn't.

Finally, Jenny was diagnosed with quadriplegic athetoid cerebral palsy. Putting it in simple terms means she has difficulty with speech and fine movements in all her limbs.

We prepared ourselves for challenging and uncertain times. The Doctors also explained she would never walk, possibly not communicating through speech and living a normal life. I think they were preparing us for a worst-case scenario. However, we refused to be downhearted and learnt to value what Jenny has, not what she hasn't got or can't do. It's a great reminder and lesson on the importance to focus on strengths.

We then began a monumental journey of discovery to find out what we could do to help and support Jenny whilst still trying to have as normal life as possible.

In our search, we discovered Hyperbaric Oxygen Treatment, Cranial Osteopathy and Brush Strokes. Hyperbaric Oxygen therapy (HBOT) is a medical treatment that supplies pure oxygen into the pulmonary system. We had to put on oxygen masks and sit in a diving chamber with Jenny, whilst inside the chamber, the air pressure is increased to three times higher than normal air pressure, making it possible for the lungs to gather more oxygen. Since blood carries oxygen throughout the body, the additional oxygen helps fight off infection while helping the body stimulate and release stem cells and growth factors. Additionally, when the body receives extra oxygen, this increase in blood oxygen will temporarily restore the correct level of tissue function and blood gas levels. We saw significant improvement in Jenny after these treatments.

We also tried Cranial Osteopathy. This form of osteopathic treatment gently encourages the release of stresses throughout the body. There are small fluctuations of movement within the body called involuntary motion, and by placing their hands on a child's body, a cranial osteopath can feel a gentle expansion and contraction of all the tissues. When these motions are disturbed, such as in childbirth, cranial osteopathy can make a child feel more comfortable. Jenny still continues to use an osteopath.

A third treatment we discovered was Brush Strokes. It is a brushing therapy developed by Steven Clarke, from work carried out twenty years ago by two Britons, Peter Blythe and David McGlown. Based on the theory that many of the problems found in children with Attention Deficit Disorder (ADD), Attention Deficit Hyperactive Disorder (ADHD) and some developmental difficulties can be related to an immature central nervous system that still exhibits reflexes which the child should have outgrown. For instance, it is understood that if a child has not outgrown the Moro reflex, it can result in unacceptable levels of adrenaline in the body, leading to hyperactivity, daydreaming, and concentration and memory problems. (The Moro reflex is the reflex in babies that makes them throw their arms into the air, and their pupils dilate and at around six months transforms into the adult startle reflex.)

The goal of brushing therapy is to mimic the movements or stimuli that should have occurred to stimulate the central nervous system's development and allow the development of the immature neurological reflexes, letting adult reactions come to the fore.

The therapist uses a paintbrush to gently stroke designated areas of the face and body twice a day for up to ten minutes for around seven months. There are twenty-five stroking exercises designed to simulate the earliest touch reflexes in the womb and seventy different movement exercises. The stroking exercises are similar to the Spanish custom of finger stroking and soothing newborn babies.

So, when most families are enjoying the bonding and the settling in of their newborn, we had the challenge of providing Jenny with the best start to her life - travelling for treatments at various sites across the UK. We still made time for plenty of cuddles and play, though!!

**So, what were the lessons learnt from this time?**
- Do your research
- Maintain a learning mindset to reduce overwhelm
- Seek out the experts and explore what others have done to be successful
- Do all you can to improve the situation
- Don't get into the blame game
- Don't become a victim
- Focus on the controllables
- Look for the right support for the situation you are in
- Make sure your children feel loved
- Build connections with your children
- Keep a positive mindset
- Look for the good in every situation
- Don't accept the situation

# Early School Years

There are plenty of outstanding schools around that support severely disabled children, but as parents, we felt that with all the support and help Jenny had already, she would do better in a mainstream school. It was what Jenny wanted too. After a short stint at Dorin Park School, we decided to put all our efforts into getting her into our local Primary School. In fact, it was the school her sister had been to and the one I had been to many years earlier. It wasn't an easy process, and Jenny's Mum fought hard to get her into a mainstream school.

We were delighted when the school agreed to accept Jenny, and she was enrolled at Kelsall Primary School, initially part-time in Year 1 and then full time in Year 2.

Understandably, the teachers were apprehensive about the enormity of looking after and teaching Jenny as it was something they hadn't experienced before.

It was upsetting for us to hear that Jenny would never be able to take any exams or achieve academically. However, after many hours of support and integration and a great headteacher, teachers and assistants, Jenny progressed through school.

It was hard for Jenny being the only one in a wheelchair. To be different at a young age is hard to grasp when all you want is friendships and to be part of a community; as a child, you want to fit in and have fun. The teachers were amazing and used the opportunity to discuss topics such as caring, diversity, disabilities, and inclusion with Jenny's class. They came to see the advantage of having Jenny at the school.

The teachers and teaching assistants around Jenny enabled her to realise that it wasn't just about playing; it was about learning too, which inspired her to learn more and get the support and care she needed to thrive in a school environment.

It was fascinating to observe how Jenny's behaviour changed from being surrounded by children with complex needs and how she responded to being surrounded by abled bodied children. It inspired her to want and achieve more out of life and not give in and allow her disability to hold her back. Jenny soon learned that she could achieve so much more herself by being resilient and seeing what other children were achieving. And of course, her determination, wit, positivity, and forever smiling face helped!

Being different and the only one in a wheelchair pushed Jenny to fight and achieve so much more. Jenny's learning was that a wheelchair shouldn't stop you; it's a tool to get you around. As Jenny progressed through Primary School, she became a well-liked and integral part of the school. It was lovely to see. There were plenty of challenges along the way, for instance, when a new climbing frame was built in the schoolyard, but it wasn't wheelchair friendly, so isolating Jenny. Imagine seeing all your friends happy and excited, playing on an amazing climbing frame, and you have to watch from the playground – tough to take when you're nine.

During her time at Primary School, I was running a Leadership Programme for Bupa called Supporting Excellence. It was a twelve-month journey for Regional Managers, and for the finale, we invited Ade Adepitan, a GB Wheelchair Basketball Player, as the guest speaker. The aim was to inspire and show what can be achieved against the odds.

As Jenny had shown an interest, I invited her to the evening. It was a pivotal moment for Jenny, as Ade told his story. Through the lessons of Ade's life, Jenny could see hope. She saw a vision of someone living a wonderful life – with all the ups and downs, of course.

Ade inspired her to take up wheelchair basketball which led to her playing at an elite level, winning the National Championships with Manchester Mavericks, representing the North West in age groups and moving into coaching. Jenny is now a level 2 coach and was part of the team that inspired and set up the Chester Phoenix Wheelchair Basketball Team with Anna Jackson. A successful and thriving basketball team, inspiring a new generation of wheelchair players.

One of the many challenges Jenny faced in year six was not being allowed to do her SATs (Standard Assessment Tests). In the end, we negotiated that she would do them, and the school would not have to submit them. Crazy school measurement system driving the wrong behaviours! Let's not go there!!

Jenny was an active member of her class and enjoyed all the school activities, sports days and school plays. On the downside, it was evident that Jenny experienced bullying at High School. Being called a retard, having doors slammed in your face, having your wheelchair called a baby buggy and boys thinking it was funny to switch off her electric chair, leaving her abandoned in the playground was very hard for Jenny to take.

Instead of letting it ruin her school years, Jenny used empathy and understanding to overcome the bullying. She used it as a mechanism to educate through discussion. She approached it by helping people understand why they did it, how it makes others feel and then working out a way forward. Jenny believes that being bullied at school has made her a better person in adult life. I would also add that she has learnt to turn emotion into learning and manage the point of choice – more about that later!

Jenny took an active role in deciding which High School she would attend. Aspects like having access to the whole school were essential to Jenny. We created a matrix of must-haves, should-haves and nice-to-haves to enable us to score each school. We visited several schools to see which would be best for her.

Jenny decided that Bishops' Blue Coat C of E School in Chester would be her first choice. Then began the battle to get her in. However, once the school had met Jenny, they were very supportive, obtaining the right equipment and creating the right environment for Jenny to succeed. The downside to this was that her teachers believed Jenny would never be capable of doing GCSEs, and she was placed in the bottom set for each subject.

Initially, Jenny had support from a nursing teaching assistant, which didn't support her needs. On reflection, what she needed was support with education. The school were great at supporting this and invited Jenny to be part of the interview process, and changes were made. They employed a fantastic teaching assistant who inspired Jenny and helped her realise she was capable of learning so much more. This support and relationship was a key element to her success.

So, a determined Jenny set out to prove them wrong. She worked hard, and her grades improved, and she was soon level with her peers. The teachers, encouraged by Jenny's determination, were so supportive and inspired her to learn more.

Jenny even became a coach and mentor for challenging pupils in the school due to her emotional intelligence and her caring way with people.

The school were very flexible and created a learner-led approach to Jenny's education. They were advocates of the 'Every Child Matters' approach. An example of this was allowing Jenny to play Wheelchair Basketball in Manchester on Tuesday evening and missing PE on Wednesday morning, and letting her have a lie-in to recover!

Through sheer determination and great teaching, Jenny managed to silence the critics and achieve 8 GCSEs – not bad for someone who was told she would never be capable of taking exams.

**Learning Points:**
- Support is key
- Relationships matter
- Determination wins
- Don't listen and believe in the naysayers
- Set goals and do everything it takes to achieve them
- Use others' negativity as a driver of your motivation

## Snowdon Adventure

**When Jenny was 10, she announced she wanted to have a great adventure, something that would challenge her. The idea came from Ade Adeptain's inspirational talk, where he shared how he climbed (crawled) the highest mountain in his country of birth!**

One of the many challenges of bringing up a disabled child is the cost implications. For example, a child's bike is around £50 to £100, but for a disabled child, who needs an adapted bike, you are looking more in the region of £2,000. Then there is all the equipment Jenny would require, such as wheelchairs, transfer devices, hoists, and electric wheelchairs – all very expensive.

We discovered many incredible charities to help with this burden, such as Kids About, Get Kids Going, and Children Today. We were very fortunate to receive help from a number of these charities.

As was Jenny's nature, she felt that she should give something back to these charities, so we developed a massive fundraising charity challenge of climbing Snowdon (Yr Wyddfa in Welsh). At 1,085 metres (3,560 feet), it is the highest mountain in Wales and England. Standing tall over the village of Llanberis, Snowdon is part of a close-knit family of jagged peaks and can offer views of Snowdonia, Anglesey, Pembrokeshire, and Ireland.

We were full of admiration for what Jenny wanted to do and very proud of the caring and determined child she had become, and we very much wanted to make this work for Jenny. For an abled bodied person, Snowdon is a challenge. For someone with quadriplegic athetoid Cerebral Palsy, it is like climbing her personal Everest!!

We knew Llanberis well having lived and worked there for several years in the early 1990s, and we believed that with the right planning, support team, equipment, and hopefully decent weather, we knew we could make it happen.

Finally, after much planning and preparation, we were ready to support Jenny's climb up Mount Snowdon. There had been a spell of terrible weather, but we managed to pick a window of opportunity in September.

Parking at Pen y Pass, there was a sense of excitement and nervousness. Had we picked something too hard? Could we do it? Will the weather hold? All these questions were running through our minds. At 0930 hours, we started the slow walk up the Miners Track. The first part is a leisurely walk for non-disabled people; for Jenny, it was a mixture of being held whilst she attempted walking, and when she became too tired, we used an all-terrain buggy. Any parent who has walked with their child when they are first learning to walk will understand how back-breaking this is!

We got to the buggy drop off point on time and then started the steeper climb. To protect Jenny, we used a backpack designed to carry younger children. We had to adapt it, but it was the most comfortable option for Jenny. With our amazing support team, Alison and John Hattersley, we worked our way up, aware of the many double-takes by fellow abled-bodied climbers!! We were tired by the time we got to the famous zig zags, and unfortunately, the weather started to turn. The wind picked up, and the last hour to the summit was hard going and very cold for Jenny. Thank goodness we had the right equipment. We had a quick break before the final assault. As we huddled together to keep warm, we debated what we should do. Should we carry on or turn around? Jenny was just as determined as ever to get to the top, so we agreed, but then we would get Jenny down the mountain as quickly as possible using the Snowdon Train. That way, we could achieve our target of getting to the top and remove any worry of hypothermia for Jenny.

At 13:30 hours, we reached the summit of Snowdon. What an incredible moment for all and an outstanding achievement by Jenny.

With the weather turning so bad and ice at the top, we had to get Jenny quickly to the middle station as the train couldn't make it to the top. Flexibility and adapting are always vital to any plan. The chip butties and mugs of tea at Pete's Eats in Llanberis were the best!

We will never forget that day and Jenny's grit and determination. It just shows what you can achieve with the right vision, purpose, determination, persistence, decision-making, and support. The joy on Jenny's face made it all worth it for me. To achieve something that many able bodied people haven't done is something to be proud of.

Jenny raised more than £2,000 for Kids About.

**Learning Points:**
- Have a clear purpose, vision and goals
- Determination and persistence are key
- Fight for what you believe in – be values-driven
- Keep your head down and work hard
- Keep curious and learn
- Prove yourself
- Use empathy
- Use adversity to make you stronger
- Build a strong support network
- Give back

## I shall let Jenny share this part of her journey with you ...

## A friend for life - Jenny's story of learning about the benefits of support for resilience

I came across a charity called Dogs for Good after a visit to Crufts one year. I watched with interest a demonstration of how dogs can help to support people with disabilities. After chatting to the staff, I suddenly realised that having a dog of my own trained in this way was a real possibility and, perhaps, more importantly, help me to live a more independent life. At the time, it was the little things that I needed help with, such as picking up items I had dropped, opening and closing doors, taking my coat off and making me feel safe in public places when I'm by myself.

I put together an application and then waited patiently for the charity to get in touch. Eventually, after a year, I finally received the news I had been waiting for, and a suitable dog was available. Because I was under the age of 18 at the time, my Mum had to become the dog's legal owner. Vera was a beautiful golden Labrador, and before we could bring her home, Mum had to go on a week's intensive training course with Vera.

Once Vera was home, everything seemed to be going well, but unfortunately, Vera started showing signs of being anxious around other dogs. Both Mum and I worked with a trainer from Dogs for Good to try and fix the problem. However, Vera got worse at pulling on the lead whenever she passed a dog, and she started to wet the bed at night. Vera went back to the trainer for three weeks to see if they could try and sort the problem out, but, in the end, it was agreed that Vera should be retired from working life. Vera was placed with a loving family as a pet dog where they had a lot of land, so she didn't have to meet other dogs. I had bonded with Vera over the time she had been with me, and so it was difficult to say goodbye. However, it was the best decision for everyone involved, including Vera.

We all felt Vera's absence after she'd left, and even though I knew it was for the best, I felt quite down that it hadn't worked out. However, I didn't have too long to wait, and within a week, Dogs for Good called me to say they had another dog available for me. I was thrilled at the news, but apprehensive at the same time in case it didn't work out again.

Nicky, a black Labrador, arrived at my house with her trainer, and we bonded straight away. Nicky was well behaved and didn't display any problems. Six weeks later, Mum and I had to take a test to prove that we knew how to control Nicky with the right commands and make sure we knew how to look after Nicky's welfare. We passed and so began our new adventures together.

Over the past ten years, Nicky has been my rock and has helped me through some very tough times. We've also shared plenty of good times too. When I had to go into hospital for nine weeks, Nicky came with me, and she intuitively sensed my needs, keeping me calm and making me smile most days. When I was at my lowest, Nicky was there lying next to me – she was such a comfort.

Nicky was even part of the bridal party when Jake and I got married. One of the best days of my life so far! Nicky was such an important part of my life that it was only natural she should play an important role on my special day. Nicky was the centre of attention, walking down the aisle with the bridesmaids wearing a special harness complete with flowers.

It will soon be time for Nicky to retire, and I am in the process of finding a new assistance dog, and then Nicky can relax and enjoy her retirement.

**Learning Points:**
- Support is essential
- Look for ideas in different places
- If things go wrong, focus on the positives
- Be persistent
- Build relationships
- You can find help in the strangest of places

# My College Years

My time at High School was coming to an end, and I needed to start thinking about what I wanted to do next. Wheelchair Basketball had become a huge part of my life, and I loved everything about it. Taking part, the camaraderie with other players and the coaching aspect of the sport. So, with all that in mind, I applied for a place at Reaseheath College to study Sports Performance at BTEC Level. My ideal job aspiration was to be a PT Instructor.

My teachers erred on the side of caution and advised me to work towards achieving a pass. However, I had other ideas. I needed to put everything I'd learned so far about believing in my capabilities no matter the hurdles and said that I'd prefer to aim for a distinction! I enrolled on level 2, and within three weeks of hard work and determination, I moved up to level 3.

During my time at College, I started suffering from stomach issues that were finally diagnosed as gluten intolerance. Despite this, I worked as hard as possible to achieve the highest grade in the class with a distinction star. An example of how believing in yourself can push you further than you'd ever hoped was on my last day of College. My final assignment was psychology, and I passed with a merit. Which is brilliant, but I didn't want just a merit. What I wanted was a distinction. So, I met with my tutor, who told me if I wanted to improve my grade, I needed to resubmit my assignment by midnight. I worked through the night to meet the deadline, and my hard work paid off when I achieved a distinction.

With the highs often come the lows. I was keen to be as independent as possible at College, and one of the ways I could do this was by taking the bus. Unfortunately, the buses weren't appropriately equipped for wheelchairs, and because my chair wasn't strapped down, it meant I had to hang on for dear life. I was terrified and worried for my safety most of the time, so in the end, I had to rely on family, friends and carers to get me to and from College.

**Learning Points:**
- Be determined
- Have a vision
- Work hard
- Be persistent

## More about the wedding!

Part of growing up with a disability makes you wonder if you'd ever have a relationship, will anyone want to spend time with you, let alone the commitment of marriage.

I didn't have too long to worry though, as I was lucky enough to meet my husband, Jake, in year nine at High School! Jake and I share the same sense of humour, and we had a lot in common. Jake proposed when we were 15 years old. I said yes without hesitation, and we were excited to share the news with our families. Everyone was genuinely happy for us, but I could tell they thought we were too young to be engaged. As we grew older, we proved our love and commitment to each other and still do today.

We were married on 4th January 2018. It was such a special day for both of us and our families. Mum pushed my chair, and Dad held my hand as we made our way down the aisle with 120 people there to share our joy. It was the most incredible feeling, and no words could adequately describe the moment as I finally married the man I loved so much. After the ceremony, I was told on several occasions that there wasn't a dry eye in the room during the service!

## Walton story:

In 2016 when I was 19, I began to feel pain in my back and leg when playing wheelchair basketball. I just put it down to a sporting injury and continued playing as normal. All seemed fine until I took part in a challenge for Sports Relief. That night I felt excruciating pain. My athetoid movements were out of control, which was very frightening. I've never known anything like it. An ambulance was called, and I was taken straight to the Countess of Chester's A&E Department.

I remember being given pain relief, including morphine, but nothing they gave me eased my pain; the only thing that gave me any relief was gas and air. As the doctors could not control my pain and movements, they decided to admit me, and I was taken to a ward. I was there for about a week while the doctors conducted scans and various tests but couldn't find anything which could be causing me so much pain.

Eventually, a neuro consultant from The Walton Centre in Liverpool, who was running an outpatient clinic at the hospital, was persuaded to visit me on the ward. He took one look at me and said I needed to go to Walton, but unfortunately, I had to wait two more days before a bed became available. I was then transferred to Walton by ambulance, and so began a regime of tests and examinations to determine what was happening.

The consultant decided to use a little-used triple-drug therapy technique, which he had only done once before in his 25-year career. They worked with the medication getting the doses right for two weeks; however, the pain and exaggerated movements continued.

As I began my third week at Walton, my medical team told me they would have one more attempt at changing the triple-medication dose. If that didn't work, they would consider putting me into a medically induced coma on the following Monday.

To my relief, the adjusted dose began to stabilise my movements and pain over the weekend. The medical team decided to observe me for another week and see how I responded. During that week, I was encouraged to get out of bed and sit in my wheelchair. As much as I wanted to get out of my hospital bed, I was extremely week after lying in bed for three weeks and had lost a lot of muscle tone. I couldn't even keep my head up. It was a distressing time not just for me but for my family to see me like this, and eventually, I was allowed to go home to rehabilitate where I would be more comfortable.

It was good to be home, and it took time, but I became stronger. A couple of months passed, and the consultant told me he wanted to start reducing my tablets. I then spent the following year trying to reduce and come off some of the tablets. However, this was not as simple as it sounds. Due to the high dose required to stop the pain and reduce my exaggerated movements, I went through withdrawal. I had to fight it using all the resiliency and determination I had learned over the years growing up with a disability.

In March 2018, the pain and exaggerated movements returned, requiring another trip to A&E, resulting in me being admitted to Walton Hospital again. My medical team decided to investigate other options, including Deep Brain Stimulation (DBS) which would hopefully control my movements. Deep brain stimulation (DBS) involves implanting electrodes within certain areas of the brain. These electrodes produce electrical impulses that regulate abnormal impulses. The amount of stimulation is controlled by a pacemaker-like device placed under the skin in the upper chest. A wire that travels under the skin connects the device to the electrodes in the brain.

In the short term, additional medication was prescribed to ease my symptoms, and I was finally diagnosed with secondary dystonia and fibromyalgia. In one way, it was a relief to receive a diagnosis, but on the other hand, I knew I was in this for the long haul. I was placed on the waiting list for the DBS operation, and after spending nine weeks in Walton, I was finally allowed to go home.

I had the operation in October 2018. After a period of recovery, I am now working with the DBS team at Walton to reduce my medication and programme the DBS settings to the point that I do not have to take any medication.

This chapter of my life has taken me through so many challenges. From really dark, emotional places filled with fear, anxiety, and depression, to finally reaching a point where I felt hopeful and full of determination.

Throughout this challenging time, I learnt two important lessons:

The first lesson was to create balance in my life and respect my limitations and the challenges of everyday life. I was newly married, and this was not the ideal way to start married life, but I found the strength not to allow my health problems to get in the way of my goals and dreams. I am certain that I could not have gotten to this point in my life without accepting help and support from my husband, family, friends, carers, and health professionals.

The second lesson I learnt, and probably the most important, is that it is essential to make the most of life and remain in the present. You can't change the past, and the future hasn't happened yet!

## My Future

I am excited about the future. My main focus now is getting back to being fit and healthy and working alongside Dad to share my story and put all the learning of my journey so far to inspire and help others become more resilient.

I believe I have much to offer to enable people to live a great life, and I am looking forward to sharing everything we have created around wabisugi and the art of resilience for everyday warriors.

Jenny's story is so powerful and continues to help teach the importance of learning and maintaining a positive attitude in life.

By now you are probably wondering how you develop your own resilience.

The next section will start that journey and share for the very first time a holistic model that decodes resilience for you.

# We call it wabisugi.

## Let's explore it together...

"LET ME TELL YOU SOMETHING YOU ALREADY KNOW. THE WORLD AIN'T ALL SUNSHINE AND RAINBOWS. IT'S A VERY MEAN AND NASTY PLACE AND I DON'T CARE HOW TOUGH YOU ARE IT WILL BEAT YOU TO YOUR KNEES AND KEEP YOU THERE PERMANENTLY IF YOU LET IT. YOU, ME, OR NOBODY IS GONNA HIT AS HARD AS LIFE. BUT IT AIN'T ABOUT HOW HARD YA HIT. IT'S ABOUT HOW HARD YOU CAN GET HIT AND KEEP MOVING FORWARD. HOW MUCH YOU CAN TAKE AND KEEP MOVING FORWARD. THAT'S HOW WINNING IS DONE!"

SYLVESTER STALLONE, ROCKY BALBOA

# DECODING RESILIENCE – THE WABISUGI MODEL

Now that we have explored why resiliency is so important, what can get in the way from our earlier years and all the learning from Jenny's story, let's discover how we can work together to improve your resiliency and performance.

To improve performance in any area of your life, you need to focus on three elements: Process, Mindset and Skills. Applying this to resiliency, you need to improve your leadership capability, your skills in the pillars and your mindset.

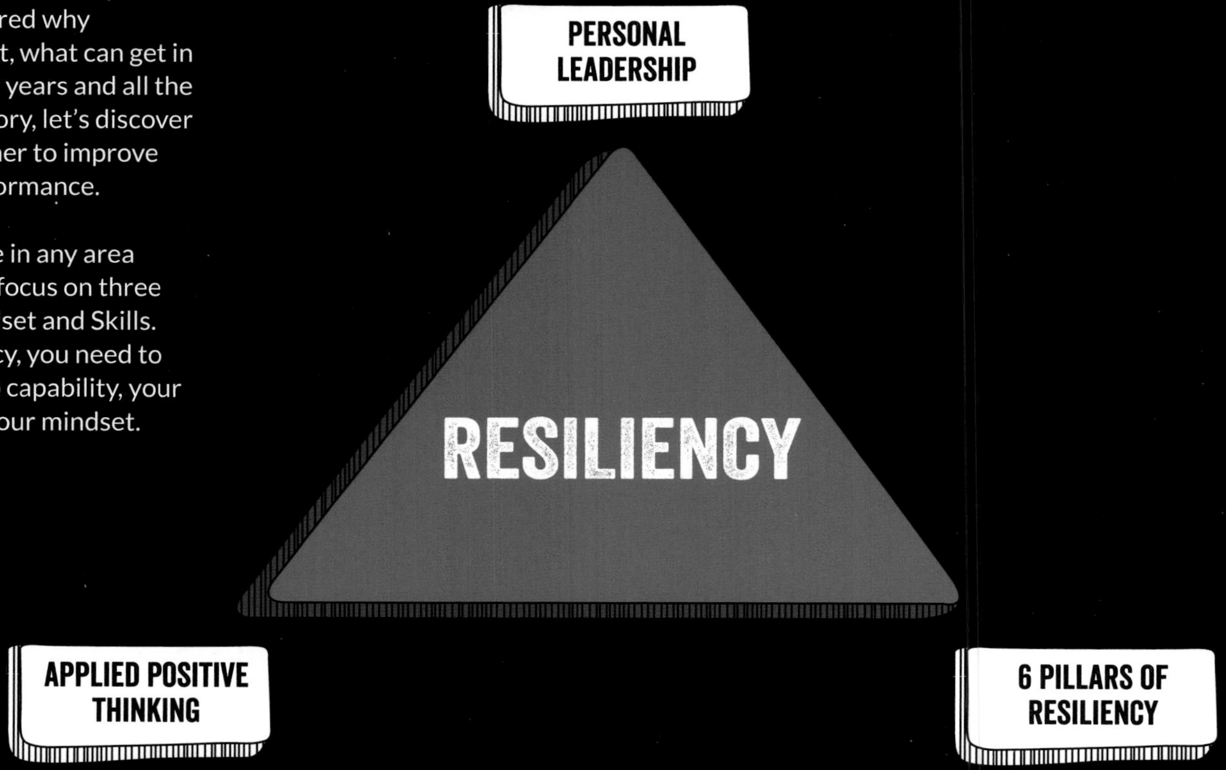

**PERSONAL LEADERSHIP**

**RESILIENCY**

**APPLIED POSITIVE THINKING**

**6 PILLARS OF RESILIENCY**

Taking all my learning from the military, Jenny's experiences, the corporate world and over 27 years of developing global leaders and exploring the latest thinking on resilience, we were able to create what we believe is the very first holistic model of resilience based on the performance improvement approach.

And we would like to share it with you now.

# wabisugi | the art of resilience for everyday warriors

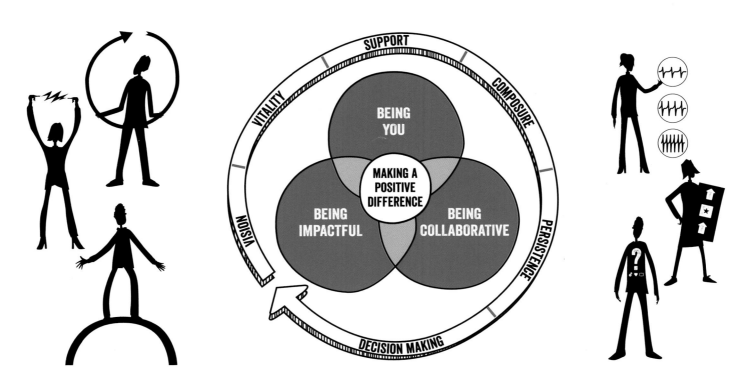

# The **wabisugi** framework

**We've created a framework that adds a range of tools and techniques you can use in developing your resiliency.**

| | VISION | VITALITY | SUPPORT | COMPOSURE | PERSISTENCE | DECISION MAKING |
|---|---|---|---|---|---|---|
| **Why** (Purpose) | Beginning with the end in mind | Creating your energy | Building your network | Choosing your emotions | Being courageous | Using head, heart and gut |
| **What** (Actions) | • Establishing Purpose<br>• Setting Goals<br>• Maintaining Agility<br>• Thinking Big<br>• Anticipating<br>• Prioritising | • Being Authentic<br>• Eating Well<br>• Sleeping Well<br>• Exercising<br>• Using Mindfulness | • Building Trusting Relationships<br>• Collaborating<br>• Embracing Diversity<br>• Building Teams<br>• Networking<br>• Masterminding<br>• Empowering | • Being Emotionally Intelligent<br>• Being Vulnerable<br>• Practicing Self Awareness<br>• Being Empathetic<br>• Self Regulating<br>• Using Red Blue Thinking | • Accepting Change<br>• Embracing Learning<br>• Being Courageous<br>• Being Curious<br>• Dislocated Expectations | • Being accountable<br>• Reflecting<br>• Taking Calculated Risks<br>• Understanding the Why, What, How<br>• Conversations<br>• Noticing<br>• Sense-making |
| **How** (Tools) | • Ikigai<br>• Identifying Strengths<br>• Personality Profiling<br>• Life Planning<br>• Game Plan<br>• Vision Board<br>• VisionIt<br>• 5 Strength Questions<br>• PERMA<br>• Wheel of Life<br>• Business Model You | • Leadership Brand<br>• Diet<br>• Sleep<br>• Movement<br>• Mindfulness<br>• Brain Gym<br>• Yoga<br>• Pampering<br>• Massage<br>• Nature<br>• Acupuncture | • 6Ps<br>• FLOWS<br>• Networking Skills<br>• Masterminding<br>• High Challenge/ Support<br>• Trust Behaviours<br>• Virtual Support Groups<br>• Family and Friends | • Emotional Intelligence<br>• Trigger Awareness<br>• Strengths<br>• Red 2 Blue<br>• Breathing<br>• Reframing<br>• EFT – Tapping<br>• Naming<br>• Anchoring | • Growth Mindset<br>• Optimizing<br>• Change Bridge<br>• Coaching Cycle<br>• SCARF<br>• Journaling<br>• Safe Place<br>• Confidence Building<br>• Self Esteem | • 5 Whys<br>• Context Mapping<br>• Cause and Effect<br>• Radiant Problem Solving<br>• Killing Risk<br>• C2E<br>• 5 Super Skills<br>• Conversation<br>• DFV Analysis<br>• 5 Questions<br>• Ease Impact Grid<br>• World Café |

Making a Positive Difference | Being You | Being Collaborative | Being Impactful

# Putting **wabisugi** into practice:

**Recognise** – Watch for the warning signs of stress and burnout

**Reverse** – Undo the damage by seeking support and managing stress

**Resilience** – Build your resilience to stress by using the six pillars

VISION
VITALITY
SUPPORT
COMPOSURE
PERSISTENCE
DECISION MAKING

## Watch out for burnout!

**You might be experiencing burnout if you:**
- Feel that every day at work is a bad day.
- Feel exhausted much of the time.
- Feel no joy or interest in your work, or even feel depressed by it.
- Feel overwhelmed by your responsibilities.
- Engage in escapist behaviours, such as excessive drinking.
- Have less patience with others than you used to.
- Feel hopeless about your life or work.
- Experience physical symptoms such as chest pain, shortness of breath, sleeplessness, or heart palpitations. (Make sure that you see a physician about these!)

**How are you going to:**
1. Get clarity around your vision?
2. Improve your vitality?
3. Get the support you need?
4. Manage your composure?
5. Become more persistent?
6. Make effective decisions?

# Developing the warrior way - Personal Leadership

Leadership isn't a position, it's a choice of actions.

We are all leaders; we all lead our own lives; we all lead others. It's not about a job title. It is about your behaviours.

It's important to think about leadership being energy. As leaders, we only have one thing that we are really in control of, and that is the energy we transmit, and we see the results through people's behaviour and body language.

And the good news is that it's always our choice what to transmit!

This transmission is a combination of our behaviours, our emotions, our thinking, and the actions we take. Then combine all these things to create the energy that people receive.

The rest of leadership is really about the other people deciding whether they want to follow us or not.

To achieve the best results, it's really important to focus on what we are in control of.

No point wasting energy on the non-controllables, as they say in sport. We are in control of our mindset, so focus on that, and results will follow.

When you think about the disruptive, volatile, uncertain, complex and ambiguous world we live in, it's easy for our energy to get depleted and for us to have nothing left at the end of the day - unless we learn a few hacks!

As leaders in today's world, it's really important to think about what you are putting in to become resilient to have enough energy to thrive. Particularly important if you like to perform at the highest level, day in, day out.

In my military days, I was taught that as a leader, when you leave a team, it needs to be better than when you joined it. It's stood me in good stead throughout my career.

It's good to think about what your legacy is.

In my role, I'm often asked what I believe leadership is really about.

One evening, I attended a celebration of a colleague's business, and the guest speaker talked about Life and Death Leadership.

He shared an amazing and very emotional story of how his 13-year-old son had saved his life whilst kayaking off the coast of Anglesey. I had a few 'hay fever moments' with watery eyes and a lump in my throat!

Firefighter Paul Rowlands, 50, and son, Joe, got into difficulty near Ynys Dulas, a small island off the coast of the Isle of Anglesey, and tried to kick their way to shore. Paul passed out due to the cold, and his son had to drag him onto rocks and try to revive him.

It was only after receiving medical help that Paul found out about his son's heroic actions.

What does leadership mean? We believe it is about making a positive difference in people's lives.

But how do you do that?

In a complex world, we have to make things simple and decode complexity into something more useable.

There are four core components for successful leadership in today's world. A real focus on making a positive difference, being you, being collaborative and being impactful.

Let's go a little deeper into each of the four core elements.

## Making a Positive Difference

I was travelling the other day with a leader of a global construction company. As we travelled the country, he pointed out the buildings he'd built, the bridges, the rail infrastructure, the schools and the roads he was part of creating.

As we drove around the UK, I was taken by his passion and excitement in describing the impact he has had on our built environment. I thought that his family, his children and his grandchildren must be very proud of him. What a legacy he is leaving.

Great leaders make a positive difference in people's lives.

Great leaders create a high-performance environment where success is inevitable. They create an environment for performance to flourish. They awaken possibility in people to deliver extraordinary results. They care, build confidence and inspire action.

**They are purpose led.**

For an increasing number of businesses and their employees, the pursuit of profit is no longer enough.

**What are you doing to make a positive difference in people's lives?**
**What's your leadership purpose?**
**What's your legacy?**

## Being You

To be able to make a real impact and leave a legacy, you have to be trusted first.

As a leader, you have to be able to lead yourself first. We need to be able to build an authentic leadership brand. Doing this will develop greater trust, better collaboration and ultimately enable your success as a leader.

There is a famous quote from Goffee and Jones in their book, "Why Should Anyone Be Led by You." They say leadership is all about,

**"Being more you, with skill."**

We talk about Inside Out Impact on our leadership programmes and how you can build an authentic leadership brand. Making a positive difference in your life and at work is about playing to your strengths, developing your skills in your strength areas, and making sure you use them.

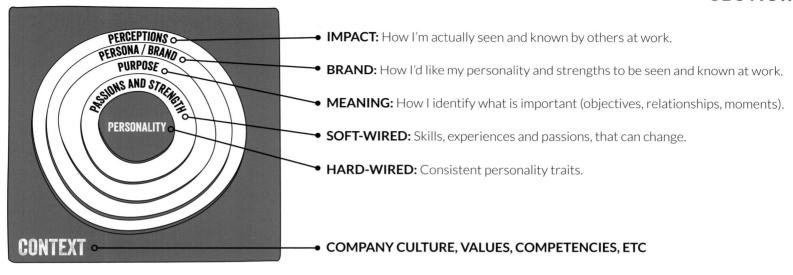

**IMPACT:** How I'm actually seen and known by others at work.

**BRAND:** How I'd like my personality and strengths to be seen and known at work.

**MEANING:** How I identify what is important (objectives, relationships, moments).

**SOFT-WIRED:** Skills, experiences and passions, that can change.

**HARD-WIRED:** Consistent personality traits.

**COMPANY CULTURE, VALUES, COMPETENCIES, ETC**

Another key aspect of being 100% authentic is around energy, and having the energy to drive change and drive business performance.

Being fit to lead, being healthy, being resilient and being mindful are important elements too.

Mindfulness is a vast topic that we need to explore in terms of being in the moment, being present, really trusting your thoughts and feelings and understanding what's really going on. It is not just inside you but also the impact you have on other people, so I think being mindful is a key element in today's fast-paced world.

**Go and practice it!**

Being healthy and having vitality are all parts of the jigsaw of being authentic. As a leader, I believe you need to be healthy and understand how to manage high levels of stress and challenge. You need to be able to thrive in a constantly changing environment. So, building your health, your strength, your fitness, your flexibility, your resiliency is a key aspect to this first truth.

So, when you are working with a leader who is being authentic, being in the moment, and vibrant, you are more likely going to follow and trust them.

# Being Collaborative

In today's world, leaders can't have all the answers. It's essential to work with people and collaborate more to achieve success.

We need to be well networked and have groups of people we can work well with inside and outside our organisations. We should feel comfortable working with remote and virtual teams. Open innovation is becoming vital for our success.

There is also a rise in the need for conversational leaders who can run great meetings and workshops. It's a skill often underdeveloped in many leaders.

How many meetings have you been in recently that added no value?

Leaders also need to be able to create high performing teams and sustain performance. They need to be able to create a team that can grab opportunities, solve problems and innovate quickly.

Leaders also need to understand the process of leadership in today's world. If we are no longer the subject-matter experts with all the answers, we need to be the owner of the process.

# Being Impactful

There is a Japanese proverb that says,

**"A VISION WITHOUT ACTION IS A DAYDREAM."**

As mentioned earlier, as a leader, it is essential to know your purpose.

You also have to know how to execute with pace; otherwise, you add no value.

To be impactful is about your productivity and your ability to influence and persuade to get things done, and being authentic and collaborative will, of course, help. The 10 Leadership Disciplines will bring all this together.
Simon Sinek tells a wonderful story of how Steve Jobs and some of his senior executives visited the Xerox Palo Alto Research Center (PARC) in the early 1980s and were shown something that Xerox had developed called the graphic user interface. With his vision of seamlessly integrating technology into our lives, he realises this fantastic piece of technology is a much better way of getting to his vision. So, he says to his executives, "We have to invest in this graphic user interface thing." And his executives say to him, "Steve, if we invest in this, we're gonna blow up our own business." To which he replies, "Better we should blow it up than someone else." And that decision became the Apple Macintosh.

Like Steve Jobs, having the willingness to make bold decisions, following your dreams, and making them happen is vital to your success.

We need to have the skills to translate strategy into meaning and inspire action, join the dots, be comfortable speeding up by slowing down, deliver through people and teams, and execute at pace.

**The key to achieving simplicity of execution involves being able to operate using four key elements:**
- The Why (Purpose)
- The What (Goals)
- The How (Plan)
- The Way (Values)

It is so easy to miss some of the elements and jump into the delivery of the task. Make sure that everyone on the team knows the why, the what, the how and the way. Try to keep it simple and make all your decisions around these four elements.

Then, with clarity in place and a team of skilled operators, you can manage by exception. Meaning you can now get on with your role as a leader rather than being hampered by routine management known as 'fire-fighting.' In other words, you can get out of their way and let them perform!

You can start to operate and set up personal routines that enable you to take control rather than be controlled by emails and crisis.

Another key element of delivering with speed is the quality of the reviews held by leaders. It is important to have regular learning reviews to keep on track. It is also a great way to celebrate success, ensure clarity, reward people, give recognition, and stimulate learning and continuous improvement.

**Delivering at Pace | Leadership questions to think about:**
- Do I translate strategy to action by giving meaning?
- Do I start explaining the 'why' first rather than the 'what' we need to do first?
- Do I hold people accountable?
- Do I ensure people are engaged and enabled?
- Do I regularly review and develop actions?

# DEVELOPING THE SIX PILLARS OF RESILIENCY

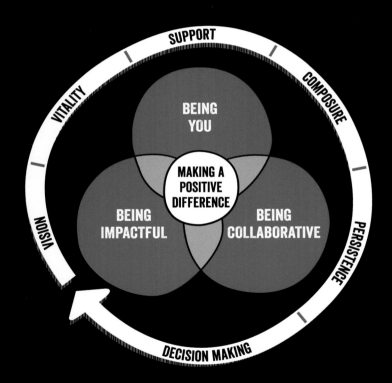

Resilience isn't just about being mentally tough. It's about how you respond to situations.

Before I introduce you to the 6 Key Pillars that have been tried, tested, and proven to help us become more resilient, let me share some of my journey and the lessons I learnt along the way.

I left school at 16 and joined the military, spending the next nine years developing resilient behaviour and mindsets to help me operate in some of the world's harshest environments, from the jungle, arctic and desert warfare and then in the toughest of all environments - peacekeeping missions. The good news is that most of the things I learnt are very simple things to do; all we need to do is turn them into habits.

A lot of what I will share is around mindset, but there are also some fundamentals that we also need to have in place that will make us even more effective.

So, let's go straight into thoughts and ideas. As you read the ideas, think about whether you have these elements in place in your life on a day to day basis.

Let's look at these mindset hacks and what you can do to become even more resilient.

# PILLAR ONE: VISION

**When I left the corporate world to start a training business, I remember not knowing where to begin.**

I watched lots of videos and listened to lots of audiotapes. I remember all the cassettes I listened to in the car. (It was the 1980s!)

I devoured all these gurus' ideas and how fantastic they were and what the great speakers of the time said I should do.

But I made a huge mistake!

The first three years of running my own business were exhausting because what I was trying to do was copy what other people were doing. Trying to be something you're not is exhausting and a waste of energy!

I realised that I didn't know why I was doing what I was doing. I just knew I wanted to get out there and train and make a difference. But I wasn't sure what my purpose was.

So, the first thing for you to think about is being clear about your vision. For me, that became very clear after a few years in business, and I suddenly realised what it was I was here to do.

For me, it's awakening possibility in people to deliver extraordinary results. If I've had a tough day, exhausted, going to bed at night thinking about whether it has been a great day or not, I can ask myself, am I on purpose? Did I make a difference today?

If I did, then I can feel really happy, and I can get more energy. I can get out of bed in the morning and keep making a difference.

Knowing your purpose is important. If you aren't clear about that, then an excellent way to think about it is to ask yourself what difference do you want to make in this world?

Once you've got your purpose in place, you need to set your personal goals. For me, that's around a number of things.

When I set my business up, I learnt that to be successful, you need to start with what you want out of life first and then work backwards to create goals that give you the life that you want to lead - making sure your goals are aligned to your purpose, and you are living your life authentically.

The more authentic you are, the easier it is. It takes an enormous amount of energy if you try to copy someone or be someone you are not.

I certainly learned this the hard way when I agreed to run a three-hour sales seminar in the UK during the evenings, and at the end of it, I was exhausted, and I didn't know why. I eventually realised that because I had to present this particular programme in a certain way, it was at odds with my way of presenting.

I immediately started to change and began to present the seminar in my own style, and at the end of the three hours, I was energised and felt more positive and guess what, the feedback I began to receive from people was a lot better as well.

So, to summarise Pillar One, being authentic is essential. Be clear about your vision; make sure you know your purpose, understand your goals and then make sure you are operating authentically.

**Tools we share later that you can use for this pillar:**
- Ikigai
- Identifying Strengths
- Personality Profiling
- Life Planning
- Game Plan
- Vision Board
- VisionIt
- 5 Strength Questions
- PERMA
- Wheel of Life
- Business Model You

# PILLAR TWO: VITALITY

**Vitality has five key components: authenticity, movement, diet, sleep, and quiet.**

Have you ever been driving on a motorway for a long time and begin to feel really tired? You pull into the service station, and as you get out of the car and walk to the food hall, isn't it amazing how more energised you feel. Movement is so important.

We're not talking about being an Olympic athlete here or having to go out and run marathons at four o'clock every morning! It is more about being aware of becoming very sluggish and de-energised because we're sitting down too much spending time on computers and responding to emails!

Therefore, it is vital to think about how much movement you can build into your day. It can be little things like walking to work, taking the stairs or parking the car further away from the entrance; all those little things add up, helping our bodies re-energise.

Find some exercise that you will really enjoy and look forward to doing in your spare time. Perhaps ask your partner or a friend to join you. It doesn't have to be a competitive or energy-sapping exercise; it's just about getting the body moving, having fun and feeling great afterwards.

The other aspect of vitality is around the fuel you put into your body.

For me, fuel is about the food, water and nutrients we put in our bodies. I could spend hours and hours talking about nutrition, but in simple terms, the food choices we make can impact our health, and it is around finding a diet that works for you and making sure you are putting the right fuel in your body. Ensuring you have the energy to perform is so vital to becoming more resilient.

The next important ingredient for vitality is to do with how much sleep you get. Allowing your body to recover after a busy day is an important aspect of a person's well-being. It's very easy to get caught up in overworking, overtraining and ignoring your body's need to recover.

Most adults require between six and nine hours of sleep per night, while some function well on less. I believe it is about finding a sleep pattern that works for you. Sleeping for me is about the body rebuilding itself and getting the energy for the next day, so it is crucial to get enough sleep. For me to feel energised and positive each day, I need between six and seven hours of good quality sleep.

The final thing on this element is around how much headspace you get. Sometimes during a business day, we can be so busy that we don't get any time to allow our brains to slow down a little bit.

When I coach people, I spend the first half-hour just listening to people offload, and their brains are going about four hundred miles an hour! We need to slow down a little bit to become more mindful of what we do.

When you combine all these elements for vitality, you could; go out for lovely walks, have meetings whilst walking, look at nature and have time to think and reflect on what's coming up for you in your mind and get some space just to be, rather than doing all the time.

To summarise Pillar Two, Vitality, there are five areas: Authenticity, movement, diet, sleep and quiet.  It's about what you put into your body just as much as what you take out.

**Tools we share later that you can use for this pillar:**
- Leadership Brand
- Diet
- Sleep
- Movement
- Mindfulness
- Brain Gym
- Yoga
- Pampering
- Massage
- Nature
- Acupuncture

# PILLAR THREE: SUPPORT

Pillar Three is all about Support. What support network do you have? It is so easy to fall into the trap of thinking leadership is about being strong, working on your own, and being the person to solve everything in your world.

This is not the case, and it is essential to surround yourself with a good support network. This can be your leadership team in a business context, it could be your peer group, and it could be the social networks or other networks you have at work. Outside of work, it could be family and friends. One of the approaches we use in our leadership training is Mastermind Groups. Getting like-minded people together for a day once a quarter to share your opportunities, issues, and challenges and then work together safely and collaboratively to solve them is really powerful.

So, what network or support mechanisms do you have in place to be successful?

Don't fall into the trap of thinking that you have to do everything yourself.

**Tools we share later that you can use for this pillar:**
- 6Ps
- FLOWS
- Networking Skills
- Masterminding
- High Challenge/Support
- Trust Behaviours
- Virtual Support Groups
- Family and Friends

# "TALENT WINS GAMES, BUT TEAMWORK AND INTELLIGENCE WINS CHAMPIONSHIPS."

MICHAEL JORDON

# PILLAR FOUR: COMPOSURE

**Pillar 4 is about composure, and this is a lot around your emotional intelligence.**

One of the things I learnt in the military was the concept around there being a stimulus - which is what you are seeing, hearing, feeling, smelling and tasting, and then there's the response. The gap between the **stimulus** and **response** is what we are in control of and is called your **point of choice.**

Imagine you are in a situation where someone is making you feel angry. Then think about the point of choice concept, and that actually, the person across the table is giving you a stimulus, and you are choosing to respond angrily. It is not the other person that is making you angry; it's you. You can't change them, but you can change your response. It really is that simple. Not easy, but simple!

So, keeping your composure and self-control is important and a key element that we used in the military to develop mental toughness - you are in control of how you feel.

Being 'tough' around the choices you make for the situation you are in is about remembering you are always in control of how you feel.

A lot of this is about composure. The self-awareness you develop will help you understand what your buttons are, your emotional triggers and all those key things that will help you understand what's happening in a given situation and make the right choices.

A key element about being resilient is that you control the situation by choosing your response.

In today's fast-moving world, nothing stays the same for long. New technology has the potential to disrupt markets and established practices, forcing organisations to adapt to new situations quickly. To be resilient in the face of change, leaders must accept the fact that change is inevitable.

They must be ready to adapt and re-evaluate situations frequently, often with limited information or time. By always looking ahead and thinking about ways to improve operations, leaders can become more resilient in the face of unexpected situations.

**Tools we share later that you can use for this pillar:**
- Emotional Intelligence
- Trigger Awareness
- Strengths
- Red 2 Blue
- Breathing
- Reframing
- EFT – Tapping
- Naming
- Anchoring

# "IT'S YOUR REACTION TO ADVERSITY, NOT ADVERSITY ITSELF, THAT DETERMINES HOW YOUR LIFE'S STORY WILL DEVELOP."

### DIETER F. UCHTDORF

# PILLAR FIVE: PERSISTENCE

Pillar 5 is all about Persistence. Persistence is like a mental muscle you can develop, sometimes called tenacity, but we like to call it bounce-back ability. When things go wrong, what is it you do to make sure that you can achieve even greater success?

In the military, it is called dislocated expectations, as it's about your choice to the situation and I think the combination of all these points made so far will help you to be more optimistic.

If you have a vision, purpose, set of goals, and a plan of action of how you get there, you can be a lot more optimistic and believe in what you are trying to achieve, which is a great thing to do.

This optimism will give you the persistence to keep going. When the going gets tough, just remember your vision and your purpose and all will be better. One of the key aspects of achieving great success when the 'bullets are flying' is the ability to keep going.

Imagine it's minus 45; you're physically exhausted from skiing and carrying a 110 lb rucksack. You're mentally exhausted and hungry, but there's a mission to complete. You've arrived at the planned rendezvous point, but there is no one there.

You were expecting hot food, a warming drink and replenishment of supplies, but there is nothing there. Your plan relied on this happening at this stage of the mission.

**How would you feel? What would you do?**

You're sat in your office looking at the latest reports from the field, and there are too many red dots for your liking. You've just read an article on how the competition is growing and that they have just won a top business award for what they are doing. Your team are just not performing as well as expected and are well behind the competition.

# "DO NOT JUDGE ME BY MY SUCCESS, JUDGE ME BY HOW MANY TIMES I FELL DOWN AND GOT BACK UP AGAIN."

NELSON MANDELA

**How would you feel? What would you do?**

It's hot, you're in Malawi, and you have a project deadline on the horizon. You are exhausted, dehydrated, hungry and have been living rough for too long. The children's nursery you've promised to build is nearing completion, but the supplies you need haven't arrived yet. Do you give up or crack on?

**Just how persistent are you?**

Dislocation of expectation is a crucial mental skill to develop for leaders in today's volatile, uncertain, complex and ambiguous world.

We need leaders who can lead through ambiguity, think on their feet and have the mindset to complete the mission regardless of what happens. They need to inspire action, build trust, ensure safety and deliver when it really matters. They need to lead without knowing the answers and, when things change, be able to stop, think and then take action - the need to be able to deliver in mission-critical moments.

This type of mindset is not developed during our education, so for businesses to thrive, we need to actively develop adaptive leaders. We need to challenge our leaders, expose them to tricky situations, get them used to being agile and creating evolving plans.

You can't teach that in the classroom. We need to develop the skills and then get leaders in a situation where they are physically and mentally challenged to see how they can perform under pressure.

You've probably heard of the term snowflake society. Sadly, we generate leaders who are not developed for today's world and the challenges they will face. The danger is that they don't understand risk, having never been exposed to it, and become overconfident and likely to make risky and costly decisions.

Let's develop our leaders to be able to deal with a dislocation of expectation.

Let's develop agile leadership.

**Tools we share later that you can use for this pillar:**
- Growth Mindset
- Optimising
- Change Bridge
- Coaching Cycle
- SCARF
- Journaling
- Safe Place

# PILLAR SIX:
# DECISION MAKING

**The final pillar of resiliency we want to share with you is about making decisions effectively.**

Taking action is a key step in removing worry and negativity.

Building problem-solving tools by building your leadership toolkit is vital. Filling it full of tools and techniques to help you decide and take action is key to your success.
The more decision making and problem-solving tools you have in your toolkit, the more resilient you can be.

One of the most powerful actions you can take in a situation where you are worrying about something is to stop and think. I call it speeding up by slowing down. Think and be mindful about what is coming up for you before you take action. Before you take action, you need to solve the problem.

Having the ability to anticipate and kill risk before It 'kills' you is a skill that can help you become more resilient. This means thinking about what potential barriers, obstacles and risks could stop you from being successful and then you need to be ready to kill them.

Make sure you take action to remove the risks you can, monitor the ones you can't remove and have a contingency in place to ensure that if they do crop up and happen, you can do something about it - have a plan B!

**Tools we share later that you can use for this pillar:**
- 5 Whys
- Context Mapping
- Cause and Effect
- Radiant Problem Solving
- Killing Risk
- C2E
- 5 Super Skills
- DFV Analysis
- 5 Questions
- Ease Impact Grid
- World Café

## Putting it all together

For your motivation and resiliency to flourish, we need all six pillars in place. If any of the elements are missing, then you'll find it harder to thrive.

There is a requirement for discipline, though. It's rather like a muscle. If I broke my arm, for example, and I was in a cast all the way up to my shoulder. My muscles would waste away as I couldn't use my arm. So it's about keeping working at it, reviewing, reflecting, focusing and making sure we become more effective at what we do. It's something that you have to keep working at.

How would you score yourself out of 10 on the six pillars of resiliency?

What action can you take to improve? What can you stop doing, start doing and continue doing?

I'm sure you will agree that there are many more resiliency elements, but getting these six in place is a good start on your resilience journey and will increase your results.

Be disciplined, and it is the difference that makes the difference.

# THE STRONGER YOU BECOME, THE GENTLER YOU WILL BE...

# APPLIED POSITIVE THINKING –
## INTRODUCING THE 12 POSITIVE HABITS

I was reminded recently about a workshop I used to run many years ago. I had gone up into the loft to put some things away as you do, and I almost tripped over a box full of acetates. Acetates, by the way, are what we used to use for teaching, and we used them with an overhead projector – a bit like the PowerPoint presentations of today. As I looked through them, I recognised an old course I used to run called Applied Positive Thinking. It was a day-long course, and it was all about keeping a positive outlook on life and being motivational and inspiring. There was some excellent information written on these old acetates, and still so relevant in today's world.

So, let's take a look at these 12 Positive Habits. Of course, the great thing about them is they are all doable if we choose to do them; they are not complicated – we just need to do them!  If we keep doing them over some time, then they become habits. They say it takes approximately 21 days to turn a particular action into a habit. We just need to focus our attention on them regularly, and they will start to become a habitual way of working, we don't have to think about them – they just become a natural part of our daily life.

The first habit is around keeping an open mind, and it reminds me of a popular quote which states, "A closed mind is as about as good as your parachute opening on the second bounce."  What a great saying, and I think it is important to keep an open mind and not get too attached to things that stop you from thinking differently.

Habit number 2 is look for the good. Things do go wrong, but if you turn that bad situation into a good situation and take the learning from it, then suddenly it isn't a bad situation anymore.

Habit number 3 is about being present. We can learn from the past, but there is not a lot we can do apart from accepting that it's happened, it's gone, and there's not much we can do about the future either because it hasn't happened yet. What we can control is the here and now.

Habit number 4 is this concept around what we call projection and reflection. You can't have something unless it is within you. You can't love someone, for example, unless you love yourself. You can't have a confident team unless you're confident first. We project what gets reflected back to us, and there are lots of different angles that we can teach you around this, which is important.

Habit number 5 is all about being grateful rather than resentful. It is about looking at your situation and being grateful and appreciative for what you have. I have many examples from my military background that I can share later on around how you can reframe things and look at the situation in a completely different way. I always say to people when they are stressed, are there any bullets flying? No, so let's rethink what's happening here and be grateful for what we have and not resentful. Feeling resentful can take over your whole body and produces the wrong chemistry.

Habit number 6 is all about playing to strengths. One of my favourite Ted Talks is by Sir Ken Robinson, who discusses how education systems and societal expectations are suffocating human creativity. During his talk, he gives an example of a young girl who is not doing so well at school, and her teacher suggests to her parents that they should take her to visit a psychologist to try and sort her problems out because she is disruptive and not paying attention in class. The girl's parents take the teacher's advice and take their daughter to see a psychologist. The psychologist sits them all down and talks to the parents, asking them lots of different questions and then turns his attention to the girl. After about 20 minutes or so, the psychologist says to the parents, "Can we pop outside a moment? Your daughter can stay here; we won't be long." Before the psychologist leaves the room, he puts some music on. They all watch through a small window in the door, and the young girl gets up and starts dancing. After a while, they all go back into the room. The

psychologist says, "Look, you haven't got a naughty child, or a disruptive child, you haven't even got a chatterbox. What you do have is a dancer." Once the girl's behaviour was treated in a more positive way, she went on to become a famous ballet dancer and choreographer and was very successful. How many other children perhaps will have had all sorts of drugs pumped into them to make sure they conform to what the schools want them to do?

Habit number 7 is all about the ability to speed up by slowing down, being comfortable with silence. There's much to be said about the power of silence, creating routines and rituals to help you make time for reflection. Whenever you are in a situation where things aren't going so well and feel out of control, it is really good to go quiet for a moment and get centred and do some meditation and think about what's going on.

Habit number 8 is all about letting go of the baggage. No one ever dies from a snake bite. What they die from is when the venom goes through the body. I think this makes an excellent analogy for our baggage, the big rucksack that we carry around with us. Negativity is heavy and takes all our energy. That's what slowly kills us; it's not the fact that it's happened it's that we have kept hold of it. I will share with you my thoughts later on and give you some fantastic tools, techniques and ideas about being more positive and ditching the baggage for good.

Habit number 9 is about point of choice. Things happen to us, the stimulus, and how we react to what has happened to us, the response. It's about how you control your reaction to what has happened – this is called your point of choice. No matter what is happening to you, you can choose a positive response.

Habit number 10 is all about how you compliment people. How do you feel when you compliment someone? It makes you feel good, doesn't it? How do they feel? We're talking about a sincere compliment here, a proper compliment from the heart, for something that's been done well. So, when you compliment people, it's a win-win situation. You feel good – they feel good. People will remember how you make them feel, not what you said. So, it is imperative to always look for the good in people. Thank you is probably the most powerful motivational words we have available to us, and we don't use them enough.

Habit number 11 is all about removing worry. 95% of our worries will never happen. 5% are going to happen anyway, so why worry? Focus on the 5% and make sure you've got some sound risk/mitigation in place to make sure that you can control those things that are going to happen.

Habit number 12 is what we call the Customer Habit. Let me ask you a question, "If you had only one customer that you could earn your living from – just one customer to earn everything you have in life, how well would you treat that customer?" You'd probably treat them well, wouldn't you? So, customer habit is this: If you treat every customer as the only one, they never will be.

## Looking at each habit in more depth ...

# HABIT #1
## KEEP AN OPEN MIND

Someone once said, "A closed mind is about as good as your parachute opening on the second bounce!"

Have you ever wondered why some people seem to be full of energy, they have a smile on their face and a sparkle in their eyes? They are always trying out new things. They go on adventures, continually learning, growing, and achieving amazing things. What they do and what they have in common is what I call an open mind.

One thing that most psychologists will agree on is that the human brain is a truth-seeking mechanism. Inside the brain, we have specific brain cells called mirror neurons, whose job is to search for positive reinforcement.

It's a bit like when you buy a new car, and you are excited to bring it home and show it off as no one else has one like it. Until the minute you go to collect it from the garage and drive it home. As you are driving along, you start to see the same car over and over again - just like yours. Everywhere you see cars the same colour, make and model! I find this fascinating as your brain is now seeking, and our reticular activation system is looking for proof that this car is good, and you see it everywhere. Of course, the mad thing is that they were there all the time, but we didn't notice them before we activated our mirror neurons.

So, this aspect of keeping an open mind is not an easy task. We are going against what our brain is trying to do, which is to prove itself right, and we need to slow down and start thinking about things differently. My eldest daughter is an Estate Agent, and she often gets asked when people are moving to a new area; they'll say to her, "Jo, what are the people like in this area?" And Jo's answer is always around, "What were people like in your old area?" And if they say they were awful, selfish, aggressive, and it's one of the reasons why they are moving to a new location. Jo's answer is, "Well, they are the same here." Someone else might say they are lovely neighbours, lovely people, we need to move to a new location for a new job, and Jo's reply in that situation is, "Well, I think you'll find the people around here are lovely as well." It is interesting about this concept of how we see things and how unconsciously we get all these biases, and we get attached to these feelings. I know there are people out there searching the internet and looking for this negativity to prove that it's a negative world. It becomes this self-fulfilling prophecy, and eventually, they become a negative person.

I remember being at a conference a while ago. One of the tutors talked about these people who are 'mood hoovers' or 'neg-ferrets' (not that I like labelling people, but it is so true). They are people that drain your energy, and you wonder why they can't see something positive in their lives!

So, keeping an open mind is really important. I always believe, and certainly when we brought our children up to help them remain curious, challenge, debate, and discuss, and I think that's something we all need to do. We've come from Old World thinking where leaders were always right, and they told you how to operate. They'd use words like appraisal and tell you whether you were right or wrong based on their preferences and their way of operating, and you were given a score based on their thoughts and ideas. We need to change all that and start using New World thinking.

To keep an open mind is to, first of all, be able to recognise when your mind is closed and resisting. For example, when you hold on to your own truth and do not try to understand another person's truth and how they see the world. Using empathy is important. Ask questions and begin to open your mind to the possibility that you might not be right. Let's face it, in today's world, it is not possible for us to have all the answers. So, we must be prepared to have a willingness to consider new ideas. Let go of any rigid beliefs we thought were sacred, and accept someone else's beliefs without criticising them.

A great way to keep an open mind is to slow down and challenge your own thinking. Ask questions and try to look at the answers in a different way. Talk to more people, read more and observe things in more detail. Why not give it a go for the next few weeks and if you like writing why not job down in a journal any changes you notice in your thinking.

I always like to go for a walk in the mornings and as I immerse myself in nature I do my best thinking. Accept that learning is an ongoing process - a key task. As the well-known saying goes, "The minute you stop learning, it is game over."

Unfortunately, the minute someone believes they are number one, they close their minds and stop learning. They believe they are the best and that they know all the answers. Then, as often happens, something changes and they are not number one anymore and they go into freefall. So, we must keep our minds agile and be open to others' thoughts and opinions.

One of the stories I heard many years ago that taught me to keep an open mind was the story of two monks going on a walk together. They come across a river, and this river is a fast-flowing river, and it looks pretty treacherous to get across. So, they are on the bank, and they are thinking about how they will cross. As they are talking and debating about the best route and how they are going to get across the river, a beautiful young lady turns up. She asks for their help, and the monks look at each other. The younger one says, "Well, we made a vow not to be with women, so what should we do?"

The older and wiser of the two decided to offer his assistance to the young lady and carried her across the river. The younger monk was furious, thinking how on earth could the other monk do that after making such a sacred vow? He joined the older monk on the other side and carried on with their walk. However, for the first hour, the younger monk cannot get past what the other monk had done. He felt so angry inside - why would this wise old monk do such a thing?

After a further three hours of silently fuming and being annoyed, the younger monk can't contain his emotions any longer and calls the older monk out. "I'm so annoyed by what you did earlier—helping that woman when we have vowed never to be in a woman's company. It's outrageous behaviour, and I am so annoyed with you." The older and much wiser monk tells him, "I left that lady on the shore over three hours ago; you are still carrying her - why is that?"

What a great example of how we can hold onto things far too long. It doesn't mean we have to blindly believe other people's beliefs all the time, it just means we should allow ourselves to look at anothers' point of view and then compare them with our own opinions.

Challenge your own thinking by listening to other people with understanding, and listen behind the message - keeping your mind open. Particularly in today's environment, where the rules change so fast, it's important to innovate and be creative.

I can guarantee your energy will increase, the sparkle will reappear in your eyes, the smile will come back on your face, and you will achieve even more that you thought possible.

Let's open up to what's happening all around us, and let's make some excellent decisions based on sound thinking and good thoughts.

# HABIT #2
## LOOK FOR THE GOOD

Remember that lovely saying, "Every cloud has a silver lining!" Fifteen years ago, I was asked to work with a Programme Director for a large global organisation. My task was to coach and mentor him to re-configure the organisational change and transformation required to take their business to the new future and achieve their vision. So, there was a lot of organisation re-design, a lot of change, many projects and programmes taking place, and my job was to help and support him and enable him to succeed.

In the early stages of getting to know each other, we had lots of great conversations and discussions, and one of the things I like to do is learn a bit about the history of the person I am coaching and mentoring. I asked him to share with me any lessons that he'd learnt along the way, and he duly shared. One of the lessons that particularly stood out for me was when he told me about a previous Programme Director in the organisation who had a great idea, took the idea to the board, sold the idea, received lots of investment and then went on to run his programme.

Unfortunately, the programme failed and did not deliver the benefits promised and did not add any value. Apart from being completely embarrassed, the Programme Director was worried and decided to offer his resignation before he was sacked. He was duly called in for a review meeting with the CEO and the Board, and as the meeting unfolded, it got to the point where he thought, right, I need to resign now before they sack me.

He took his letter of resignation out of his pocket and handing it to the CEO; he said, "I believed I'd initiated a programme that would deliver the results required. Unfortunately, it hasn't, so please accept my letter of resignation."

The CEO paused for a moment and, looking at him, said, "Well, why would I accept that? You've just had the most expensive personal development course out of anyone in my organisation. If I allow you to resign or you get sacked, then where would you go? The Programme Director thought about this for a while and said, "I'd probably, if I'm honest with you, go to one of our competitors and work with them because obviously, I need to provide for my family."

The CEO said, "Exactly, so why would I want you to go there? What I'd like you to do is take the learning from this experience. I know it's been hard. It's been hard for all of us. We know it's failed; you will need to work hard on your brand and your reputation within the organisation but let's take these lessons and apply them. Obviously, if you do it again, then we'll have another conversation."

If you think about what happened in a bit more detail, the CEO was looking for the good in the situation, and yes, the Programme Director made a bad decision. It failed, but the CEO believed in the Programme Director, and he would deliver outstanding value in the future.

So, Habit #2 is about always looking for the good in a situation. However, when I say this, I don't mean going around in a fantasy bubble where the world is always an amazing place! What I mean is finding a balance between healthy optimism versus a little bit of reality.

Another way of thinking about it is for us to create environments where people can thrive. I truly believe in awakening possibility in people and creating a healthy balance. To create the energy, we need the right balance of cortisol and adrenaline. These hormones get us ready for the fight or flight situation, which drives us to do things. However, if we overdose on cortisol and adrenaline, we suffer from adrenaline fatigue, which harms the body. Therefore, it is essential to get the chemistry in our bodies correctly balanced with an equal amount of DHEA, serotonin, testosterone, oestrogen – all the positive chemicals. It is the same with our mindsets, we must make sure that our mindsets are balanced. So keep reading and I will share with you some ideas and thoughts about how we can do that.

When I think about my grandparents, I know from their many stories of their past that they'd gone through some challenging times, including World War II for six years. Imagine that, six years of rationing, hardship, your loved ones being away at war and having to bring the family up by yourself and having some really tough decisions to make.

Certainly, in the cities, having to send your children away to safety must have been hard for them. My grandparents had these amazing sayings; they'd say things like, "Every cloud has a silver lining." Do you remember that one? Every cloud may have a silver lining, but you have to go and look for it. You still have to go and look for the good. Another one is, "Things happen for a reason," Do you remember that quote? And "All things pass." They were very wise, and used these great quotes or mantras if you like, that helped them through challenging times. One of the things we can do when we are looking for the good is to think about the things we are saying to ourselves. Ask yourself, am I creating a healthy balance? Am I getting some reality in place? Am I focusing on the positive things?

I remember years ago, working with a call centre to help them look at their engagement, motivation, and teams' success. One of the things I do when working with a team is observing them working. You can imagine the environment, can't you? There were many call agents around the room, with floorwalkers and team leaders going around listening to calls. I noticed that the team leaders would always go around and only comment and give people feedback when something wasn't right. Obviously, they need to do that for compliance and ensure the customer is getting the right information. Unfortunately, it was creating quite a negative culture where the staff were never good enough. To help them achieve that healthy balance, I suggested that the team leaders catch their team when they are doing good work and reinforcing their good work with a compliment. Which, by the way, is another habit we'll talk about later on.

The Pandemic of 2020 - 2021 is an excellent example, with many organisations stopping to reflect and think about their purpose. Do they need such a big Head Office in the future, when working from home has proved to be very successful? When we are experiencing a challenging situation, do we stop and think? Instead of drowning in the situation's negativity, do we ask ourselves what this situation will give us? What opportunities do we now have to change the way we do things?

This ability to be able to stop, think and reflect is so important. Otherwise, we end up on the hamster wheel, on automatic pilot and nothing changes.

It's a well-known fact that things can go wrong even if we are good at something. It can even be the simple things that can turn a good day into a bad day unless you change your thinking. I was making myself some toast one morning, and whilst I was buttering the toast, it fell onto the floor. True to form, the toast landed on the buttered side. Instead of allowing the situation to ruin my breakfast, I heard my Grandma's voice saying, "Things happen for a reason," and I remembered that I was trying to cut down on my carb intake, so I threw the toast in the bin and ate a healthy banana instead!

Think about some of the things that are going on in your life at the moment. What are the positive things that perhaps weren't before? Are you able to spend more time with your loved ones, because you are working from home, giving you more time to think and reflect.

# HABIT #3
## BE PRESENT

## "THE GREATEST GIFT YOU CAN GIVE SOMEONE IS YOUR TIME, YOUR ATTENTION, YOUR LOVE, YOUR CONCERN"

### JOEL OSTEEN

Over the past 26 years, I have been fortunate to work with some of the best leaders in the world, and as I worked with more and more leaders, I began to look at their most common traits.

What are the things I see in all of them, and what do they all do? One of the things I have noticed that great leaders do is they are always in the moment, always present – they have this ability to be able to switch off from all the distractions they have in their lives and things that are going on around them and be there in the moment.

One of the greatest gifts we can have as human beings is to give people our full attention. Of course, the challenge we have is that in today's world, we are bombarded, aren't we with lots of information, emails pinging in, our mobile phones ringing, and we can become distracted.

There's a common misconstruction that multi-tasking is an essential part of what Leaders should be doing. They should have multiple jobs on the go - keeping all those plates spinning! This is a myth. After much research and certainly the research I have been reading, it has been proven that the brain is not wired that way. Our brains do what is called

task shifting because we like the chemical called dopamine, and dopamine is like a reward. If we start doing things, we get an immediate reward. It is why we are distracted by our phones, aren't we and Facebook, LinkedIn, and all other forms of social media. They all have their benefits, and it is fantastic that we can communicate with people, but we need to manage it effectively.

There is a fantastic book, which I highly recommend, written by David Allen, called Getting Things Done: The Art of Stress-free Productivity. In his book, he writes about a five-stage process workflow methodology. He tells us that a chain is only as strong as the weakest link, and if you don't perform properly at each stage, then your productivity will suffer. So, it is important to collect, process, organise the results, review and then engage in the work you need to do; in other words, simply do. Using this methodology is a very effective way of working.

What are some of the things that we can do to remove these distractions to enable us to be in the moment? All the people that I know that can do this are more productive. I know from research that up to about 40% of wasted time is around us, flitting from one task to another, trying to unsuccessfully multi-task, spreading ourselves too thinly, and unable to finish anything. We need to break down our to-do list into more manageable tasks and just focus on one thing at a time, making us a lot more productive and successful. If you are going to have a conversation with someone, have just that. Sometimes when I am running a virtual meeting, it is apparent some of the participants are distracted, surreptitiously checking their emails, and are not in the moment. So you ask a question, and all you get is silence because they suddenly realise you are waiting for them to answer! Then you hear them say, "Could you just repeat that for me? I didn't quite get what you meant."

I think it is essential in today's world to commit to being in the moment, to give your full attention to the task at hand. If we want to go for a walk in nature, let's just go for a walk in nature – let's remove the headsets, put the phones away and actually really be there in the moment to take in the beautiful sights and smells of nature and just be, be in that moment and value it. Because when we do that, we are recharging our bodies, and we are going to be a lot more effective, and we are going to get a lot more from it, a lot more learning, and a lot more success.

Another key skill for being present is our ability to listen effectively. I often find that when I am listening, sometimes my mind will drift off to what someone else had said perhaps an hour or so ago, which will cause me to miss something crucial

in my current conversation. To avoid this from happening, one of the things I've learned and trained myself to do is to hold state, be present, and use a technique called Rapid Repeat. In my head when I'm listening to someone, I repeat what they are saying. If I can repeat it in their accent, that's being even more focused and more powerful.

Something else you can do to be present is to remove the trap of having back-to-back meetings. I repeatedly hear people saying I've had such a busy day; I've been coaching all day, I've been in virtual meetings all day, it's been back-to-back. It sounds that they are trying to massage their ego, aren't they, telling themselves how important they are but not being effective. You can't go from one meeting to the next meeting to the next meeting and be effective. Because the first 10 minutes of the next meeting, you are still thinking about the previous meeting. So, build in some time for reflection, finish one meeting, and then get yourself in the right state to start the next meeting. It is about creating headspace. In the first 15 - 20 minutes of every meeting or coaching session, it is clear that most participant's minds are racing so fast that they cannot be in the right mindset for a productive meeting or really powerful coaching and mentoring session. So, the first 20 minutes of any session, just allow for that unwinding and slowing down process to happen. Once they start to relax and be more present, that's when we can start asking the challenging questions.

I remember once having to take a flight to run a workshop for a client. Unfortunately, the flight was delayed, so I headed to the airport bookshop to peruse the shelves. I chose what I call 'an airport book' because it was a quick read. The book was called The Present by John Spencer.

I do a lot of scanning when I start a new book, and as I flicked through and got to the end, I thought, "What was that all about," so when I finally boarded the plane, I read it more thoroughly and made some notes. It was a fascinating read, and although it was a short book, it was very powerful. It taught me that when you are looking for the secret of life, then there is only one present, and the present is this:

The past has happened. There's not much we can do about that apart from taking the learning from it. It's useful to review backwards and start to learn from things that have happened to you. That's the past.

There's also the future, but there's not much you can do about that yet, apart from predicting what might happen. You can, however, use the learnings from the past to plan for the future.

What you can control is the present, and that's what the book was all about. The secret to a successful life is in the present, being in the moment. That was the gift John Spencer's book gave me, and I'd encourage you to think about it yourself - is it something you can do?

THE PRESENT

# HABIT #4
## BE AWARE OF PROJECTION AND REFLECTION

**Two things that can occur in our interactions with others are reflection and projection. Reflection is when experiences reflect back to us from others that show us aspects of ourselves, and projection is where we externalise aspects of ourselves onto others that aren't actually them.**

As leaders, we have to think about what we are projecting on to others. How does it affect the things we achieve, our minds and the positivity we have? I came across this concept when I worked with a consultant I found difficult to communicate with. There was something about him. He was a lovely guy, very clever, and we did some great work together, but there was something about the way we worked, which I felt was very difficult.

I didn't trust him completely, there were lots of checks and balances in place, and there was something deep down inside me that was saying I wasn't sure about this person. What transpired was after much reflection, I realised that this consultant looked remarkably like a primary school teacher I had all those years ago when I was in infant school. I thought that was fascinating. Here's this person I am not trusting, and it's not them that's the problem; it is me.

All because of a memory I had tucked away over the years telling me, "Don't trust people like that."

This teacher was quite nasty to me from what I can remember and gave me a hard time, and wasn't very kind. So, subconsciously I was projecting my dislike and lack of trust on to the consultant I was working with, all because of a distant memory of how someone made me feel. There's me thinking it was the consultant that was the problem and all the time it was me! So, I changed my mind-set, and since then, we've done some fantastic projects together, and we are more self-aware and connected.

What I would like to do is share my take on it. I'm not saying I'm right, by the way, I am just saying that this is how I understand it. It dips into the world of the law of attraction, and spirituality and all those fantastic concepts. It is quite a complicated topic, but for me, it is quite fascinating. I am still learning about it, but it is something that resonates with me.

For me, Leadership is all about energy and the frequency you transmit.

My first career was in the Military, and I spent a lot of time setting up communication systems to operate in both war and peacekeeping situations. You can't fight a war or keep the peace without excellent comms, and that's all about having the right frequencies and the right equipment to be able to transmit and receive and get the messages through with clarity – in the moment and when you need them.

I think the same applies to outstanding Leadership. Leadership is a transmit and receive process. I am transmitting my energy, and you are receiving it, and I'm getting that message back. You then choose if you connect with it, then you'll choose to either follow me or not – it's as simple as that.

However, it can sometimes get complicated when a leadership team in an organisation sets the tone and what that means is the frequency that the leadership team is projecting to the people working for them. For example, if they project a lack of care and a lack of trust because they can only think about profit and their bonuses, they will not fully engage the people working for them.

I believe this concept of projection is something we can control, and once we understand it, it is really powerful, and this is where the law of attraction comes in.

Do I understand the law of attraction? No. Do I understand how it works? No, but I do know that what you project out, you will receive.

It is often said that you can't receive love unless you love yourself. So, if you love yourself and project love, then you'll get love back. That's a great concept because it means it is in our control. If I wanted to have a positive life, I have to project positivity. There are lots of people out there who look for negativity. They are like a negativity magnet, aren't they, mood hoovers who scroll through the internet looking for negativity and then feed on it. Then, surprise, surprise, they receive a lot of negativity back.

If you look for the good, you'll find it. Whatever you look for, it'll get bigger. So, I think that concept is very similar – all these habits are linked. This whole concept of being aware of the frequency you are transmitting is fundamental to living your best life.

One of the techniques we love to use and is very successful is working with horses to give the leaders feedback about how they externalise themselves.

We use horses because they are prey animals, and their 'flight' instincts can be non-judgemental feedback mechanisms for humans. Horses sense and respond to a person's intentions, emotions, and thoughts that are conveyed subconsciously through body language, which means they are susceptible to any form of energy a person may be projecting. Even the slightest shift in approach can make a huge difference to the horse. For example, if you are transmitting any negative energy, they will see you as a threat. If you are transmitting authentic and positive energy, they will be content to work with you. The same principle applies to people. If we transmit the right energy, the right positive mindset, the love, the care, and empathy, people will receive that and follow. If you choose to operate negatively, then that's what you will receive back. It is important, therefore, to learn to be mindful of the frequency you are projecting.

Has this ever happened to you when you walk into a room? There's a couple who are sitting together, not speaking, but you can feel their energy. You can sense there's been an argument of some kind going on before you had arrived. The energy they are creating is palpable.

I have seen this happening in big corporate organisations where they are going through a transformational change process, and the senior leadership team have to go through the process first. They finally reach the moment when they understand and are on board with all the changes, and then they are ready to move on to the implementation stage. So, they hold a big conference and invite everyone in the organisation to share this massive change that is about to take place. The senior leadership team are on the stage, projecting positivity and excitement. The problem is, however, the audience hasn't caught up yet. The audience is stuck on, "Oh my god, what's going on, have I still got a job, what's going to happen, how am I going to pay the mortgage, what will people think about me if I lose my job."

What needed to happen in this situation was for the senior leadership team to have shown some empathy with the audience and been more aware of the process they needed to go through first, just as they had done. The audience would have had time to catch up and be more open to the changes that were to take place.

Let's transmit at a frequency of care, collaboration and support. Be mindful of the frequency from where you are operating, and make sure you are operating from the right frequency.

# HABIT #5
## BE GRATEFUL

**"GRATITUDE IS THE FAIREST BLOSSOM WHICH SPRINGS FROM THE SOUL."**

HENRY WARD BEECHER

To understand Habit #5 and the importance of being grateful, I'd like to start with a lovely story I heard a while ago, which illustrates the importance of being grateful. In Africa, many years ago, there was a farmer who inherited his farm from his father. He was the youngest son, and all his brothers had gone off to find work and settle into profitable careers, and the youngest brother wishes he hadn't been chosen to take over the farm from his father. He has a young family, and farming is challenging, and he will have to work hard to provide for his family.

The young farmer becomes very resentful. He then hears about people in other parts of Africa finding diamonds and becoming fabulously wealthy, which only adds to his frustrations. This resentfulness starts taking over his life, so eventually, he decides to sell the farm, take his family, and search for these diamonds that everyone else seems to find. He doesn't want to work hard anymore, and he just wants to find one of these diamonds and be successful, have lots of money and live a great life.

He sells his farm to a young couple whose greatest wish is to bring up their family on a farm because they love nature and working outside and do not mind the hard work.

The farmer goes off with his family in search of his fortune. Unfortunately, it is quite a sad story as he eventually dies destitute, having never found any diamonds.

Back on the farm, the new farmer is out toiling in the fields, and a beautiful blue stone catches his eye in the river, and he thinks to himself that it would make a wonderful gift for his wife. She works hard keeping house, supporting the family and bringing up the children, and he thinks it would be a lovely way to show his appreciation. He picks the stone up, goes home, and the next morning at breakfast presents her with the stone. His wife is delighted by her husband's thoughtful gift and decides to put the beautiful stone on the mantelpiece.

One day there's a visitor to the farm. He is invited in and offered some food and drinks. They take him into the lounge, and they sit down and start talking. The visitor notices the stone on the mantelpiece and nearly falls off his chair. Recovering himself, he explains to the farmer and his wife that what was sitting on their mantelpiece happens to be one of the largest diamonds he's ever seen.

I think that is such a remarkable story, isn't it when you think about it. The resentfulness of the original farmer drove him away from where his success was all along. It is so easy for us not to value the things we already have. You often hear the phrase, 'The grass is always greener on the other side.' We have to recognise that everything we need is usually right under our feet. We just don't always notice it!

Here are seven tips that I've learnt over the years that have helped me to move away from being resentful to being more grateful in my life.

### Tip #1
Start the day by being grateful. What are the positives in my life? It's a great way to start the day. There's a great video on YouTube of a commencement speech given by US Navy Admiral, William McRaven who tells his audience that the first task of the day should always be to make your bed. "If you want to change the world, make your bed first."

I think that's great. My challenge to that would be to be grateful first, spend some time thinking about what you're grateful for and then make your bed!

### Tip #2
Spend a bit of time noticing when you are complaining. How much of your time do you spend complaining about things? It is hard to be grateful and complain at the same time.

Focus on being grateful rather than being caught up in complaints and issues and the problems of the day.

It's a bit like when you go on holiday and find one thing wrong with the hotel, you then start looking for what else is wrong with it and forget to be grateful for the fact that you are on holiday having a great time. We are complaining about all the things that are going wrong.

There is a great story about Gandhi where he is about to board a train. He slips and one of his sandals falls on to the train tracks. He quickly takes the one he's still wearing and throws it to the floor near to the sandal he lost. Someone said, "Why did you do that?" Gandhi answers by saying, "One slipper is no use to me, but two will be good for someone else."

### Tip #3
Keep an open mind. Read, listen to audiobooks, think about what other people do, and open your mind to what is fantastic in our world and listen to some of the success stories out there, how people have gone through difficult times and have still managed to become successful. The more we read, the more we observe, and the more we look at things, the more grateful we can become.

**Tip #4**

Appreciate what you have. During my time in the military, I spent some of that time in Beirut during the war in the 1980s. I noticed when the bullets were flying; there was debris everywhere and all sorts of horrible things going on, including the bombing of the American Embassy. There were all sorts of tragedies going on around me, but I noticed that children were still playing in the streets; even though they could have been shot by sniper fire at any time, they were having a great time. They were just happy playing with their friends as if nothing was wrong.

I always use that as a bit of a wake-up call when I think I'm stressed and I'm starting to feel resentful, finding life hard and having a bit of a 'pity party'. I use this comparison with other people in other situations. I ask myself, are there bullets flying, no – so I have got nothing to complain about, let's be grateful for what we have and that we do have a wonderful life. There are people out there who have a tougher life than us, so be grateful and appreciate what you have.

**Tip #5**

Slow down. Start to notice all the beauty around you. Whether that's in buildings, nature, or people and actively start to find things of beauty. When you start to see it, you will start to realise how great your life is.

**Tip #6**

Handwrite a letter. I can remember when my Grandparents retired to Spain in the early 1970s. The only way we could communicate with them was through letters. Letters are so powerful, aren't they? Science has linked expressive writing to a better mood, reduced stress and an improved sense of wellbeing. So, get off your computer, find some good quality writing paper, your favourite fountain pen and write a letter by hand. Tell the person you are writing to how much you love them, how much you care for them and how much you support them.

**Tip #7**

Remove the gossip. There's nothing remarkable about gossip, is there? It hurts people, it is not good, and it is not the right thing to do. We should just remove it – it's quite simple, just stop gossiping.

# HABIT #6
## PLAY TO YOUR STRENGTHS

**"SUCCESS IS ACHIEVED BY DEVELOPING OUR STRENGTHS, NOT BY ELIMINATING OUR WEAKNESSES."**

MARILYN VOS SAVANT

**If I were to ask you what your strengths are, you'd probably find it quite tricky because it is not easy to understand what you are good at because it's natural for you. It is something you find easy.**

What some people find to be difficult and challenging; others might find it to be easy. I will explore its significance and how it helps you, and how sometimes our past experiences don't help us focus on our strengths.

How many of you, for example, have been involved in appraisals? After a fantastic year, there's that one moment in the year that you made a mistake, and the whole conversation seems to revolve around that one mistake rather than the great successes you had.

It's rather like if I were a football coach, for example, and my star striker is in for their performance conversation. We sit down together and we have a conversation where I say, "Look, you've had a fantastic year, and I'm pleased with how you've come back from injury. You're a brilliant team player, and you've scored some great goals, so well done. However, I've noticed that when we are on the training pitch and it is your turn to be in goal, you aren't very good are you?

So, what I've decided to do is send you on a goal keepers course." Now, if you were a sports coach of an elite team, you wouldn't do that, would you? What you'd probably do is identify what your star striker is really good at and send them on courses to improve on that.

The real performance comes from when everyone is focused on using their strengths and are allowed to put their strengths to good use.

In my book, Leadership Laid Bare, I wrote about a wonderful story I'd heard several years ago, and it takes us to China, to the mountains and a small village. In the village lives a family in a house with no running water. Every morning, the devoted father woke early before anyone else, and he would pick up two pots with one of those sticks you put across your back, and he would walk for a mile and a half to a river to pick up clean water. He would walk down the same path, collect the water in the pots, turn around, and then come back the same route every morning.

However, this story is really about the two pots. One day the pots get talking to each other. Unfortunately, one of the pots had a few cracks in it and water would leak out of it, so the pot was only a third full by the time the man had gotten back from the river to home. On the other hand, the other pot was nice and shiny and brand new and had no cracks in it and didn't leak.

During the conversation, the perfect pot said to the cracked pot, "You seem to be a bit down at the moment. What's wrong?" The cracked pot was upset, and given the opportunity, poured out his sadness. "I feel humbled in your presence and admire how perfect you are. Every day we come back, and you are still full of water. I'm only a third full if I'm lucky. I feel like I'm broken and not providing as much value as you do."

The perfect pot thought about this for a while and replied, "Well, have you ever noticed that on the way down, there are some beautiful flowers on one side of the path, and have you noticed that the man picks some flowers for his wife every single morning? He brings the flowers back, and he puts them in a vase and his wife comes down to breakfast and sees the flowers and is really happy."

The cracked pot said, "Yes, I have noticed this. It makes me feel great seeing the smile on his wife's face every morning, "And have you noticed that the flowers are only grown on one side of the path?" Asked the perfect pot. "Yes, it is strange, isn't it?" Replied the cracked pot. "Why do you think that is?" Asked the perfect pot.

The cracked pot thought about this for a little while and realised that what was happening was that as they were walking back from collecting the water every single day, the cracked pot was watering the flowers and making the flowers beautiful. On the other side of the path, where the pot was not leaking, there was no water, and no flowers grew.

I think that's a beautiful story. When we think about it, we don't always value what we've got, and we don't spend enough time thinking about our strengths. We use several tools in our business to help leaders understand this. We use training questionnaires, such as Strengths Profile. Strengthscope is another tool, and all the work that Gallop do as well. What is it that gives you energy, what do you find easy, what perhaps are some of your unrealised strengths?

When we are building teams, one of the things we do is make sure that people are playing to their position, they are using their strengths, and we build on their strengths and make sure they use more of their strengths. I think that is an excellent outlook on life; indeed, when teams and individuals and leaders use their strengths, they will be a lot more effective, and the research backs it up.

We use a body of thinking called Appreciative Inquiry to help teams understand their strengths. It is incredible what people can do when they are focused on the positives and apply their strengths in any situation. They are going to be really successful, aren't they?

# HABIT #7
## SPEEDING UP BY SLOWING DOWN

Special Forces operators have a slogan when it comes to urban combat:

## "SLOW IS SMOOTH. SMOOTH IS FAST."

**You can be efficient, but are you effective?**

In today's world, we hear about this fast-paced world we live in, but I think many people confuse fast-paced with being busy. We spend our time focusing on efficiency rather than efficiency and effectiveness. I know many people who think they are extremely busy, believe they are operating at a fast-pace but are not being effective. They might be efficient, but they could be efficient in doing the wrong things!

My father used to race motorbikes in his younger days, and my uncle used to race motor cars. As a young child, I used to listen to their stories of them racing around the UK. What was very interesting from their conversations and certainly something that I've learned was that a trend started to appear from a conversation. Every time they lost a race, it was because they were going too fast. Quite ironic when you think about it. As a young boy, I thought racing was all about going as fast as you can all the time.

Obviously, as an experienced racer, you need to know when to go fast, but you also need to know when to slow down, and I think in business, it is very easy to get caught in the 'hamster wheel effect' of being busy all the time. When was the last time you saw on a meeting agenda, whether virtual or face-to-face, time put in for reflection? Or the evaluation of ideas?

It tends to go from, here's a problem, quick debate, here's the solution. Agree on an action, and off we go. How many times have you been to a meeting, for example, where you've agreed to something in the meeting, the pressure is off, you've gone away and reflected on it and thought, actually in hindsight, it's probably not the right thing to do. "Have you been there?" We all have, haven't we? It is fascinating how we get caught up with this whole thing around being efficient and doing lots of things when we can be more effective by actually slowing down. For example, when things go wrong – when do they go wrong?

Do they go wrong when you are in control, calm and collective? Or is it when you are very busy? It's when you are busy, isn't it? So, if you think about it, a good time to stop and reflect would be when you are busy. However, this is probably the one time we don't stop, do we? We just get busier and busier and are not as effective as we could be.

So, what I learned from my father and uncle was that you could speed up by slowing down and win more races by knowing when to go fast and knowing when to slow down. Slow in, quick out, which is something the racing world talks about when going around corners.

Understanding this can be very useful from a business point of view. One of the challenges we have nowadays is that people find it very difficult to cope with silence. Whenever there is a pause or some downtime, people immediately reach for their phones or start replying to emails. I like to make sure I allow for some reflection time to think.

I was once asked to bring a European team of leaders together for some team bonding. They all worked in separate locations and needed to spend some time together, getting to know each other and understand each others' ways of working. They all travelled separately and arrived at the venue at different times.

Observing each one as they arrived, I noticed a pattern. First, they got acquainted with the venue and discovered where the refreshments and facilities were located. Then each one of them found a quiet place to sit down on their own to check their emails. They all knew the purpose of the event, and they were all aware that they didn't spend enough time together, yet they were quite happy to go and work in isolation! I think that's an interesting trait we can have where we get caught up with all the busyness, we've always got to be doing something, we have to do our emails straight away, I've got to be doing

this, I've got to be doing that, and I think we need to start re-educating ourselves. I am hoping, particularly with what we are all experiencing now with the virus and lockdown, we are starting to see the value of speeding up by slowing down and understanding the importance of reflection.

A handy tip from me would be to build reflection time into your meetings. If you are running a virtual meeting, it is a good idea to start by sharing your problem. Do some brainstorming about the actual problem itself first, and then have a little break. Taking some timeout gives everyone a moment to reflect and check-in with each other whether or not everyone is tackling the right problem.

Once that is all agreed, you can go to the next stage to generate some ideas and solutions to solve the problem. Again, have another break, reflecting on the suggested solutions, then come back together, and look at all the ideas and decide which ones you will take and make them into really big ideas and implement them into the business.

I think this whole concept of speeding up by slowing down is something that can reap benefits within your organisation if we have the courage to do it. I hear so many people talk about back to back meetings, whether virtual or before we got into lockdown, face to face. It is impossible to be effective with back to back meetings, and we need to build in some more time and be comfortable with silence.

I have read that mindfulness, meditation and silent retreats have been used to rehabilitate offenders with positive results. By using mindfulness to re-programme, participants felt less-stressed, and could manage their emotions and behaviour resulting in fewer prisoners re-offending.

We should never be uncomfortable with thinking and reflecting. Let's start to put reflection times into our agendas and start to think about how we can do that effectively and for people to be comfortable with that.

A few years ago, I was running a workshop where an organisation were having a problem with reaching their sales targets. It was a tough environment to work in but what they found was their sales team weren't hitting their target of 20 calls a day, so the senior team got together, had a debate around the problem, and their solution was to double their target to 40 phone calls a day. I remember thinking, why have they done that?

When we started to dig deeper, we found that using a telephone, something they have used for many years, is probably not what the customer wants anymore. The last thing they want is a telephone call because that would interrupt their work. So, we began to look at the problem differently, and maybe they should use different mediums such as texts or emails, or maybe think about the timing of the phone calls. Make fewer phone calls but make them more effective.

By slowing down and looking at the problem differently, there was a dramatic improvement.

Another example was when I ran a project management training programme for a company. The senior team explained that the project manager was not very good. He was not delivering the benefits they needed, so they wanted him to train and learn more about project management techniques.

When we explored the root cause of the problem we found that the project manager was good at managing projects. He knew how to run projects and had been running them for many years.

The real root cause was the culture of the organisation and how the projects were governed. It was bureaucratic, and it was a bit like walking through treacle, making it extremely difficult to get decisions made. So, rather than running a project management training programme, we spent some time looking at the culture and the organisation's leadership style and how to govern projects to move away from the bureaucratic way of doing things. The organisation noticed the improvement almost immediately and were delighted.

# HABIT #8
## REMOVE BAGGAGE

**"JUST BECAUSE YOU HAVE BAGGAGE DOESN'T MEAN YOU HAVE TO LUG IT AROUND."**

RICHIE NORTON

**Imagine the effort of carrying around a 15kg rucksack all the time!  Emotional baggage feels the same!**

Can you imagine going to the gym and picking up a big 15kg weight and holding it in your arms and spending your whole life carrying around such a weight?  It is going to be draining and exhausting, preventing you from performing at a higher level.

All the emotion we store away comes from our previous experiences. I like to think about emotion as energy in motion, and energy in motion around the body is good when it is positive energy and positive emotions. Still, the challenge is when emotions get stuck in the body, and we carry them around. Let's have a look at what I believe happens.

We are born with a set of DNA which is the body's hardwiring. I believe what happens is our many experiences during the early stages of our lives can be either good or bad. I had the pleasure of coaching a chief exec of a company once. I can't divulge who, but he told me that one of his pivotal moments was being sent away to boarding school at a very young age and how that had dramatically affected his life. He eventually realised what a negative effect it was having on him.

These emotions and experiences wrap themselves around our hardwiring and form what we call our belief systems. Our beliefs form early on in our lives, and we carry these around as we grow into adulthood. It's a bit like having a computer programme installed in us at an early age. Our beliefs trigger our self-perception and are the window to how we see the world. Do you see the world as a great place, a positive place or do you see it as a really dangerous place, and you are very negative?

The second thing that our beliefs drive is our self-talk, our inner voice. I find it interesting when I'm coaching people around presentation skills. Most people know how to prepare a presentation, and they know what they should be doing. Still, something prevents them from giving a good presentation. It is their inner voice saying, "It's going to go wrong, the audience won't like it, you will forget your words." This self-talk, the negativity we put ourselves through, will then start to impact us.

A final thing that our beliefs will drive is our feelings, how we feel in a particular situation. If we return to using our presentation skills as an example, and during a meeting, someone says to you, "I've got this fantastic opportunity for you! I'd like you to present to the Board of Directors next week, is that ok?" Now for some people, that feeling will be fantastic, but for other people, it's going to be an absolute nightmare, they wouldn't sleep for a few days, and they'll find it hard because our belief system drives it, and whatever has happened to us in our early lives.

So how do our beliefs form? Our brain operates as a truth-seeking mechanism. For example, when you were at school, you are asked to go to the front of the class and read aloud from a book. Let's say that time you do it well, and the class clap and the teacher said well done. From that moment on, after such a positive experience, every time you stand up in front of an audience, your brain finds enough evidence to form a belief system that tells you standing up and talking in front of a group of people is a good thing to do.

Then, let's say you stand up and read aloud to the class and get it wrong for whatever reason. There are a few chuckles in the class, and the teacher says you must try harder and you find it a negative experience, making you feel uncomfortable and unhappy. What happens from that moment on, your brain will start looking for proof that presentations are a bad thing. I see it all the time when people are fantastic in meetings when they are sitting down, but they can't talk the minute they have to stand up. It's almost as if their brain has switched off.

Both situations, positive or negative, are caused by our belief system, triggering our body's chemicals. A positive experience releases the feel-good chemical dopamine, which switches on your brain. A negative experience will release stress chemicals around the body, such as cortisol and adrenaline, which will switch off the brain's thinking part because you are in a fight or flight situation.

A self-fulfilling prophecy occurs as no matter how brilliant your presentation is, in the moment, it goes horribly wrong. As you get to the end of the presentation, you think to yourself, "I knew this would happen", and so re-enforcing your belief that standing in front of a group of people is a bad thing to do.

There's a lot more to it, of course, but put simply, our belief systems create our self-perception of the world. It is not the truth; it is just what we perceive to be the truth. Driving the physiology and chemistry inside our bodies, which then operates how our brains work, driving our behaviour, and the action we take to achieve the results we get, enforcing the belief system. It is really important to understand that all happens so that we can do something about it. There are lots of different techniques to help you start to reprogramme your belief-systems. For example, Tapping, EFT, and NLP techniques are really useful for you to explore.

One of the things you can do is try and control your physiology. It's what athletes do. They will control their physiology through their breathing. You might believe you are in a bad situation, but it is still possible to trick your belief-system that you're not stressed.

You'll get a flood of positive chemistry inside your body which means the brain switches on, and you can remember the things you want to say in your presentation.

Each time you challenge your belief-system by doing this, you will slowly build up your confidence, and you can move from your comfort zone into your stretch zone.

Because of the negative things that happen to us, our emotions get stuck in our body. Many people have ailments, challenges and pains in their bodies, and physically there may be nothing wrong. It is an emotion that is trapped, and we have to get rid of it. There are many ways of doing that, of course, through exercise, dance, running, getting out in nature, massage, acupuncture, just getting the body moving again – there are loads of different techniques that can help you.

Many breathing techniques work well to move any unwanted emotions. When people are stressed, you can see where their emotion is locked in their bodies. I've seen people doing presentations where they are holding on to different parts of their body, and when you feed it back to them, they have no awareness of doing this.

So, no matter how deep the emotion is stored, we can change how our belief system works by understanding it and removing it.

# HABIT #9
## POINT OF CHOICE

**"BETWEEN STIMULUS AND RESPONSE, THERE IS A SPACE. IN THAT SPACE IS OUR POWER TO CHOOSE OUR RESPONSE. IN OUR RESPONSE LIES OUR GROWTH AND OUR FREEDOM."**

VIKTOR E. FRANKL

This habit is all about stimulus and response and the importance of controlling the gap between the two. What tends to happen through our experiences, we create connections where certain stimulus will trigger a certain response. How many of you have been in a situation like the one I had, where I can remember taking my children back to the primary school I went to as a child, and the smell of the school took me right back to when I was young. It felt so real, as if I was there at their age going to school. It was still that deep in my memory. I can have situations where certain tonalities of people's voices can trigger responses inside me. I'm sure we've all got different triggers, depending on our life experiences, and they all come from this whole concept of protecting ourselves and making sure that we are safe and survive. These memories get wrapped up in our belief system and our emotional part of the brain.

It is important, therefore, to remain positive and to protect ourselves. Making sure we understand what triggers the negative responses and knowing what to do about it. For example, if I hear a certain tonality of a voice that triggers a response in me that causes a fight or flight response, I am trying to protect myself from that tonality. That may not be the truth. It might not be the best response in that situation, so we need to understand a little bit about physiology and how that works and make sure we don't get hooked into our memories, enabling us to control our situation in a more positive way.

Point of choice is a really useful technique to understand. How liberating would it be if you found yourself in a difficult situation and that you could remain in control? This is where mental toughness comes in. No matter how terrible the situation, you can always choose to respond positively. If you can do that, you are more likely to be successful in life.

So, how do we do that? Let's understand physiology first, and I will share a tool with you that I learnt a while ago, which looks at the sympathetic and parasympathetic system in the body.

**High Energy Needed (Accelerator)**

PEAK ZONE

ANGRY ZONE

Feel Great

CHILL ZONE

CAN'T BE BOTHERED ZONE

Feel Bad

**Not Much Energy Needed (Brake)**

The diagram shows on the vertical axis the high energy needed (sympathetic) and low energy needed (parasympathetic) situations. The horizontal line measures our feelings from positive to negative.

The way our physiology works is depending on the stimulus we are receiving through our senses.

The vagus nerve is the nerve that wanders around the body collecting lots of information. It links to our heart, gut and brain. It's rather like a super-highway. It tells the body immediately if we need high energy or low energy.

A stimulus that puts you in a high energy situation floods your body with adrenaline. If the stimulus is perceived as negative, the stress hormone cortisol will be released, putting you in the 'Angry Zone'. We are ready to fight, flight, freeze or flock!

In sport, they call it the 'temper tank.' You might have heard athletes saying that I just 'tanked that'. 'I didn't run as well as I could because I tanked it.' What has happened is that they have allowed their feelings to get into this high energy and negative situation. It has changed their physiology, making them unable to run as fast as usual because of the chemistry inside their bodies.

With training and awareness, we can control our feelings to boost our coherence and resiliency.

In the bottom right, 'can't be bothered' quadrant, I'm relaxed, and I have a low heart rate, but I am in 'victim mode,' which is not a good place. It's where you feel very sorry for yourself. I might be relaxed, but I've still got plenty of cortisol in my body.

I have low energy down in the bottom left quadrant, 'the chill zone,' or what athletes would call the 'recovery zone.' My parasympathetic system is driving different chemistry, opposite to adrenaline. I'm relaxed, feel great, and I am feeling positive.

The Angry Zone and the Can't be Bothered Zone are quadrants where we don't want to be. Sometimes known as Red Thinking, when we are either in a situation where our body is saying we're stressed, we will be putting on weight, the logic part of the brain is switching off, you're not thinking clearly, and overwhelm sets in.

The dangerous part of this is that the body adapts, and this can become the norm. We think living over in the negative area, high or low energy is normal. This is not a good way to live because we are full of bad chemistry. We want to move over to the chill zone or the peak zone, which is often called Blue Thinking. If I were a competing athlete, I'd want to be in the high energy/peak zone – my maximum point of success.

If I trained hard and needed to recover, I'd want to be in the low energy/chill zone – nice and relaxed, full of great chemicals such as DHEA, Testosterone, Oestrogen, and Serotonin.

Interestingly, our feelings control which side we are on, so being in control of your response and feelings is very important, and the key point about this is that the gap between each response is your point of choice.

So, how do I choose my feelings?

One of the key things we need to do is make sure that we are not forcing ourselves into the angry or can't be bothered zone by doing too much or setting unrealistic goals. We are not allowing these negative feelings to fester in our body, allowing this unrealistic way of working, causing adrenal fatigue, which is the outcome of being in the negative zones for too long.

One of the things you can do is, of course, is to stop and reflect on that and think about what is it I need to do?  Be more aware of what is happening around you and think to yourself, "Am I allowing this to happen? Am I overwhelmed? Am I doing things I don't want to do?" Start to get comfortable with discomfort and acknowledge that you can get back to positive thinking when you are in a negative situation. If you are setting challenging goals for yourself, break them down into little steps, and, more importantly, make sure you are still living your values.

What we can do is develop a set of breathing techniques. Many of the breathing techniques we know will take us from the negative areas and start to bring us into more positive areas. Heart breathing is a concept developed through a body of science researched by the HeartMath Institute. There are some great tools and techniques that can get us back into coherence.

Creating a Coherence state puts you on the left-hand side of the chart, 'Peak Zone' and 'Chill Zone'. Our heart variability is nice and smooth, and over on the negative side, it is rough, and we need to control that. Breathing is a great way to calm down the vegus nerve and change the information going around the body and get us into that peak zone. You can see it in athletes, can't you when they change the way they think and feel just by using a breathing technique before the race. They are getting themselves from the chill zone to the peak zone so they can operate at their highest level.

I hope you found this stimulus and response concept useful, and remember we control the gap between the two, our point of choice. I think that it is liberating and positive. If we know that it doesn't matter what happens to us, we can always respond positively, which is always our choice.

# HABIT #10
## COMPLIMENT PEOPLE

**When was the last time you received a really sincere and genuine compliment? One that made you feel fantastic.**

When you compliment someone, you feel fantastic, and the person you've complimented feels fantastic too. Win-Win!

I'd like to share with you some really interesting research I read about a few years ago and have since researched myself. I wanted to understand the importance of complimenting people and how important it is for a leader to do that.

I am always amazed when hearing about the number of people furloughed during COVID lockdown, and their leaders and managers haven't even bothered to contact them.

Much of the research I have read shows that a sincere compliment will trigger the same part of the brain as giving someone cash!  Imagine if I had a big suitcase of cash and gave it to you that would trigger a certain response in a part of your brain that will make you feel really good.

The chemical that does this is called dopamine, which is known as a reward chemical. It can get us addicted to things like the likes and shares on social media because we like that instant gratification, and it is one of the things that gets us hooked.

So, dopamine is a really important thing, and when you think about leadership, leadership is around making sure people can perform. Dopamine helps the brain be more effective and helps all the connections that allow access to more information.

Certainly, from a learning point of view, when we are developing training programmes, we want to create the right environment and get people to slow down and get into the right state of learning. One of the things we do is always make sure people understand the benefits they will get from the training programme. Because when you trigger off that reward circuitry and flood the brain full of dopamine, it makes the brain cells sticky and more likely to be susceptible to learning.

I can relate to that. I remember surviving school because I am lucky to have a good memory, so I revised hard and managed to pass all my exams. That was until I joined the military. I soon realised that learning had a purpose; if I didn't learn how to use a particular piece of equipment, I might die, and suddenly the reward of not dying became a catalyst for proper learning.

There Is a Japanese phrase called Hado, meaning vibration or wave motion, founded on the premise that all things are in a state of vibration. I found this fascinating.

After some research, I learned that the study of Hado was first explored by Dr Masaru Emoto, a Japanese scientist who realised that the molecular structure in water transforms when exposed to human words, thoughts, sounds and intentions.

In his book, The Hidden Messages In Water, Dr Emoto shows us how water exposed to loving and compassionate words, pictures, and sounds results In aesthetically pleasing physical molecular formations.

If the water was exposed to fearful and unpleasant words, pictures, and sounds, it created disconnected and disfigured physical molecular formations.

I would highly recommend reading his book. The photographs alone of the crystals formed when exposed to the different intentions are pretty amazing!

Questions began buzzing around my mind. If water is affected by words, intentions and energies, what about human beings, who are made mostly of water?

There is something special when connecting with the water, and certainly, from a personal point of view, I feel at home when I am around water. Many of my hobbies involve water in some way, such as sailing, paddle boarding, canoeing, and windsurfing. I can feel lonely and trapped in a high rise flat in the middle of a city, but I never feel like that when I'm in nature and close to water.

Whether it is scientifically proven or not, Dr Emoto's research resonates with me. Suppose you are vibrating positivity and love instead of hatred and anger. In that case, the energy you emit in your organisation has to make a difference, and that difference is really important.

Let's think about the damage that leaders cause when creating negative energy in their organisations - always shouting at people, constantly finding mistakes in people's work. I have seen this behaviour many times when I've worked with teams, and the way we iron out the problem is by using a fantastic tool called Appreciative Inquiry. It is a tool for teams to encourage them to come together and focus on positivity. The team then start to grow and build and be more successful.

So, habit #10 is all about the importance of complimenting people. Merriam-Webster defines a compliment as an "expression of esteem, respect, affection, or admiration." Research tells us that a genuine and heartfelt compliment on a person's performance or work profoundly impacts their self-esteem and productivity. So, if you see a colleague doing something well, tell them.

On the flip side, of course, is being able to receive compliments. A great tip to help you respond to feedback is to say, "Thank you," remain quiet and breathe. There's no need to justify it or deflect it, just take it on board. Whether it is positive or negative, it amounts to the same thing. I repeatedly observe people's inability to accept a compliment when I am coaching people to give great presentations and watch them on the stage. The audience is enjoying the presentation, there's big applause at the end, yet the presenter can't get off the stage quickly enough rather than graciously accepting their reward for a great job.

# HABIT #11
## REMOVE WORRY

**"IF YOU CAN'T SLEEP, THEN GET UP AND DO SOMETHING INSTEAD OF LYING THERE WORRYING. IT'S THE WORRY THAT GETS YOU, NOT THE LACK OF SLEEP."**

DALE CARNEGIE

I'd like to share a wonderful way to address your worries. I discovered it a few years ago now, but I think it is very apt for today's world, and I hope it will help you think about being in the right mindset to thrive in these tough conditions we are facing at the moment.

It can be very easy to allow cortisol and adrenaline to take over our natural stress responses in difficult situations. That initial kick is great to get us thinking and then to take action. However, if we allow it to overwhelm us and take over our bodies, it is very easy to get to the point where the thinking part of our brain switches off. We can't think and make good decisions, leading us to start worrying. Once this happens it is a downward spiral, and we get ourselves into blame or victim mode. It becomes impossible to think clearly for ourselves, our families or in the workplace.

So, back to the 'worry box'. Find yourself a good solid cardboard box. A shoebox would be perfect. Empty the box of any packaging and carefully cut out a hole in the top of the box, enough to post a piece of paper through. If you feel creative, you can decorate the box and on the side of the box, write the words, 'The Family Worry Box' in big letters. This box will be for the whole family to use whenever you catch yourself worrying, overwhelmed, or have feelings of guilt. Before writing anything, stop and reflect for a moment.

Think about what's going on, and then write it down. Then place the piece of paper (the worry) inside the box and then carry on with your life.

Choose a day of the week that all the family can get together. We find a Sunday evening works well for us and don't forget to add tea and your favourite cake!  Remove the lid from the Worry Box and empty its contents on to the table. Encourage the family to read the bits of paper and ask yourselves how many of the worries happened and how many didn't?

It is a well-known fact that at least 95% of our worries don't happen, and the other 5% will happen anyway, so why worry?

A 'Worry Box' is a wonderful technique to bring your family together and help you to focus on everything that is positive in your life. Also, supporting your loved ones and making sure everyone is making the right decisions.

In these troubled times, let's switch off from all the scaremongering in social media and focus on what matters and what matters is you, your family, your loved ones, your community and the people around you. Let's go out there and show some care - let's make a big difference.

# HABIT #12
## DEVELOP THE CUSTOMER HABIT

**"TREAT EVERY CUSTOMER AS THE ONLY ONE, AND THEY NEVER WILL BE."**

GRAHAM WILSON

I mentioned at the start that these habits are in no particular order. They are all extremely important. It's about making sure we use them as much as possible and remain positive even in tough conditions.

Habit #12 is all about Developing the Customer Habit. So, what is the customer habit? Let me share with you an example and what happened to me when I received an email from a holiday company. We were due to go to Centerparcs for a family celebration; all our children's birthdays are in May (good planning!) So we like to do something special for them and this year we had decided to go to Centerparcs for a long weekend and enjoy some good quality time together.

But unfortunately, the Pandemic happened and Centerparcs had to close. I was impressed with how well they had set up their website to help with their customer enquiries. They are a huge company spread all over the UK and Europe and as you can imagine they were inundated with people wanting to know what would happen to their holidays. What was impressive about it was Martin Dolby's message, their CEO, which was how they will support their customers through the process of changing their holidays or cancelling them. You could either click a button for a complete refund, no questions asked or click another button to re-book.

They had removed their re-booking fee and all you had to do was type in your name, booking reference and the name of the Lodge you'd like to stay in and the date. Click confirm and that was it - all done.

So, within no more than 5 minutes, everything was sorted out. I was a little bit apprehensive about it beforehand. Still, I quickly changed my viewpoint when I checked my emails and guess what; there was the booking confirmation from Centerparcs, and they were looking forward to seeing us there. What a fantastic process. Even though it was an online experience, it certainly was a positive and trustworthy process I went through. For me, I thought that was so powerful.

As leaders, we have many different customers, and it might be that your team are your customers. You could argue that your family are your customers. Certainly, a senior team that you report to might be your customers.

Imagine if you could only earn all your income from one person. How are you going to earn your income from that one person? How well would you treat them? You'd probably treat them well. You'd do everything you could to make sure they are happy and feeling positive and having a trusting and good relationship.

I shall explain customer habit in a little more detail. When you treat every customer as the only one, they never will be – imagine the difference that's going to make. Sadly, what we tend to do is prioritise people don't we. Sometimes, we see it where clients are sending teams to Successfactory, and the client says, "They are only Team Leaders." At Successfactory, everyone is important to us – we don't differentiate. We treat everyone the same, with the same experiences – always looking to succeed.

There's a wonderful concept by Seth Godin around Purple Cow. If you haven't already read his book, I'd highly recommend it. Imagine if you are driving around with your family and your children are in the back of the car and suddenly, they see some cows in a field, and they've never seen cows before or certainly haven't seen brown cows before. They are talking about it, "look, daddy, look, mummy, there are some cows in the field, and they are amazing."

As they continue their journey, they see the same cows over and over again – suddenly you stop talking about them, and I think that's the same in today's world; there is so much information out there. There's so much similarity. How do you make yourself stand out and be remarkable?

Suddenly, as they drive past another field, there is a purple cow. Imagine what the children will say! "Look, look, there's a purple cow, what's that! Suddenly there is something in front of them that is different and remarkable.

In the British Military, one of the first things they talk about, certainly when they are training officers, is around the importance of serving, how you serve in leadership, and serving your teams. It is important to understand that you are there to serve your team and every person in the team as a leader.

Challenge yourself to make your interaction with everyone you deal with completely remarkable. Obviously, from a commercial point of view, we need to get the balance right to make sure the business is still commercially viable while giving a remarkable customer experience.

One of the concepts I am passionate about is a concept called Value Innovation, which comes from asking the right question. Suppose an organisation suddenly has a situation where they are struggling. Money is tight, and they're not making as much margin as they should do. It is very easy to get caught in the trap of cost-cutting. However, as soon as this happens, the customer experience is no longer remarkable.

The problem is we don't always ask the right questions. I call this 'And' thinking which is how you get the best of both worlds. The right question to ask is, "How do we add more value to our customers while reducing our operating costs." What this does is drive innovation.

Innovation, for me, comes from having a customer-focused mindset. Look at what your customers are struggling with, what will they need now and, in the future? If organisations start to think in a customer-focused way and exceed customer expectations by delivering what customers need, they are the organisations that are going to be successful in the future.

Remember, if you treat every customer as the only one, they never will be.

# IN SUMMARY

We've been on a journey together through the key elements of improving your performance – personal leadership, the 6 pillars of resiliency and applied positive thinking.

Combining these three elements with the wabisugi framework enables you to develop outstanding resiliency.

We started by sharing what can get in the way.

We then shared a model for personal leadership with you, which will stand you in good stead in the future. It's all about making a positive difference by being you, being collaborative and being impactful.

The 6 pillars of resiliency will give you plenty to think about, and the toolkit that follows this section will help. Make sure you revisit it regularly.

And finally, we looked at how you keep a positive mindset – even when the going gets tough.

You now have a great framework to ensure you can be the best you can be and positively thrive in today's world.

Now take time to explore the warrior toolkit. We hope you enjoy it!

## You are a wabisugi warrior!

**PERSONAL LEADERSHIP**

**RESILIENCY**

**APPLIED POSITIVE THINKING**

**6 PILLARS OF RESILIENCY**

# wabi**sugi** | the art of resilience for everyday warriors

# WARRIOR TOOLKIT

| | VISION | VITALITY | SUPPORT | COMPOSURE | PERSISTENCE | DECISION MAKING |
|---|---|---|---|---|---|---|
| **Why** (Purpose) | Beginning with the end in mind | Creating your energy | Building your network | Choosing your emotions | Being courageous | Using head, heart and gut |
| **What** (Actions) | • Establishing Purpose<br>• Setting Goals<br>• Maintaining Agility<br>• Thinking Big<br>• Anticipating<br>• Prioritising | • Being Authentic<br>• Eating Well<br>• Sleeping Well<br>• Exercising<br>• Using Mindfulness | • Building Trusting Relationships<br>• Collaborating<br>• Embracing Diversity<br>• Building Teams<br>• Networking<br>• Masterminding<br>• Empowering | • Being Emotionally Intelligent<br>• Being Vulnerable<br>• Practicing Self Awareness<br>• Being Empathetic<br>• Self Regulating<br>• Using Red Blue Thinking | • Accepting Change<br>• Embracing Learning<br>• Being Courageous<br>• Being Curious<br>• Dislocated Expectations | • Being accountable<br>• Reflecting<br>• Taking Calculated Risks<br>• Understanding the Why, What, How<br>• Conversations<br>• Noticing<br>• Sense-making |
| **How** (Tools) | • Ikigai<br>• Identifying Strengths<br>• Personality Profiling<br>• Life Planning<br>• Game Plan<br>• Vision Board<br>• VisionIt<br>• 5 Strength Questions<br>• PERMA<br>• Wheel of Life<br>• Business Model You | • Leadership Brand<br>• Diet<br>• Sleep<br>• Movement<br>• Mindfulness<br>• Brain Gym<br>• Yoga<br>• Pampering<br>• Massage<br>• Nature<br>• Acupuncture | • 6Ps<br>• FLOWS<br>• Networking Skills<br>• Masterminding<br>• High Challenge/ Support<br>• Trust Behaviours<br>• Virtual Support Groups<br>• Family and Friends | • Emotional Intelligence<br>• Trigger Awareness<br>• Strengths<br>• Red 2 Blue<br>• Breathing<br>• Reframing<br>• EFT – Tapping<br>• Naming<br>• Anchoring | • Growth Mindset<br>• Optimizing<br>• Change Bridge<br>• Coaching Cycle<br>• SCARF<br>• Journaling<br>• Safe Place<br>• Confidence Building<br>• Self Esteem | • 5 Whys<br>• Context Mapping<br>• Cause and Effect<br>• Radiant Problem Solving<br>• Killing Risk<br>• C2E<br>• 5 Super Skills<br>• Conversation<br>• DFV Analysis<br>• 5 Questions<br>• Ease Impact Grid<br>• World Café |

Making a Positive Difference | Being You | Being Collaborative | Being Impactful

## Putting **wabisugi** into practice:

**Recognise** – Watch for the warning signs of stress and burnout

**Reverse** – Undo the damage by seeking support and managing stress

**Resilience** – Build your resilience to stress by using the six pillars

**Watch out for burnout!**

**You might be experiencing burnout if you:**
- Feel that every day at work is a bad day.
- Feel exhausted much of the time.
- Feel no joy or interest in your work, or even feel depressed by it.
- Feel overwhelmed by your responsibilities.
- Engage in escapist behaviours, such as excessive drinking.
- Have less patience with others than you used to.
- Feel hopeless about your life or work.
- Experience physical symptoms such as chest pain, shortness of breath, sleeplessness, or heart palpitations. (Make sure that you see a physician about these!)

**How are you going to:**
1. Get clarity around your vision?
2. Improve your vitality?
3. Get the support you need?
4. Manage your composure?
5. Become more persistent?
6. Make effective decisions?

# PILLAR ONE:
# VISION

IKIGAI
IDENTIFYING STRENGTHS
PERSONALITY PROFILING
LIFE PLANNING
GAME PLAN
VISION BOARD
VISION IT
5 STRENGTH QUESTIONS
PERMA
WHEEL OF LIFE
BUSINESS MODEL YOU

# IKIGAI

**What is it?**

Ikigai 生き甲斐 ("a reason for being") is a Japanese concept referring to having a direction or purpose in life, providing a sense of fulfilment towards which a person may take actions, giving them satisfaction and a sense of meaning.

**How do I use it?**

To find this reason or purpose, experts recommend starting with four questions:

**What do you love?**

**What are you good at?**

**What does the world need from you?**

**What you can be paid for?**

Finding the answers and a balance between these four areas could be a route to Ikigai for Westerners looking for a quick interpretation of this philosophy. But in Japan, Ikigai is a slower process and often has nothing to do with work or income.

# IDENTIFYING YOUR STRENGTHS

### REALISED STRENGTHS

Perform well • Energising • Higher Use

**USE WISELY**

### UNREALISED STRENGTHS

Perform well • Energising • Lower Use

**USE MORE**

### LEARNED BEHAVIOURS

Perform well • De-energising • Variable Use

**USE WHEN NEEDED**

### WEAKNESSES

Perform poorly • De-energising • Variable Use

**USE LESS**

**What is it?**

Strengths Profile is an assessment tool that helps you identify your strengths. It measures energy, performance and use. It categorises 60 attributes into 4 areas:

**Realised Strengths** – attributes that you perform well in, energise you and you use frequently

**Learned Behaviours** – attributes that you perform well in but do not energise you and use varyingly

**Weaknesses** – attributes that you perform poorly in, do not energise you and use varyingly

**Unrealised Strengths** – attributes that you perform well in, energise you but use infrequently

**How do I use it?**

Contact a registered practitioner who can administer the online questionnaire and give a structured feedback session to help you understand the model and what the report is saying.

We are more than happy to work with you on this.

# FACET5 PERSONALITY PROFILING

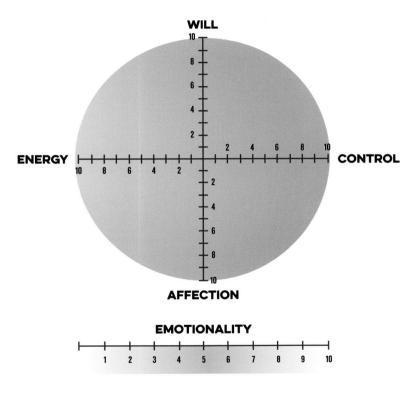

**WILL**

**ENERGY**

**CONTROL**

**AFFECTION**

**EMOTIONALITY**

1   2   3   4   5   6   7   8   9   10

| WILL | CONTROL | ENERGY | AFFECTION | EMOTIONALITY |
|------|---------|--------|-----------|--------------|
| Determination<br>Driving<br>Purposeful | Discipline<br>Responsibility | Vitality<br>Sociability<br>Adaptability | Altruism<br>Support<br>Trust | Anxiety<br>Apprehension |

## What is it?

It is a psychometric tool that we use for building self-awareness, emotional and social intelligence which is based on the Big 5 Model of Personality developed by Norman Buckley.

There are 5 Facets: Will, Control, Energy, Affection & Emotionality and 13 sub facets (Determination, Confrontation, Independence, Discipline, Responsibility, Vitality, Sociability, Adaptability, Altruism, Support, Trust, Tension, Apprehension).

Each person who completes the survey will receive a "rating" against each of these Facets and sub-facets which is then mapped against a chosen "norm" group giving you a profile. This profile is placed to the nearest "family" of 17 families to show preferences of behaviour, communication, leadership and working styles grouped together in a confidential report.

## How do I use it?
## Contact us to get your report done online.

Once you have your report and have had feedback:

- Read through the report noting any points you agree with and don't agree with.
- Share the report with your friend, partner, spouse and ask them to give their opinion (how does the report represent you?)
- What does the report highlight for you in your role?
- What does this mean for you?
- How can you make some changes?

# LIFE PLANNING

| IN 12 MONTHS TIME<br>I will be... | | | |
|---|---|---|---|
| **GOALS**<br>(The specific 'What', breaking it down) | **STRATEGIES**<br>(The general 'How' – your preferred approach) | **MAKING IT HAPPEN** | |
| | | **Actions & Ingredients**<br>(Resources you'll need & types of steps to be taken)) | **Measures**<br>(How you'll recognise & measure your progress) |
| | | | |
| | | | |
| | | | |
| | | | |
| | | | |
| **MY DEFINITION OF DAILY SUCCESS** | | | |

**What is it?**
A template to guide you through developing a plan to achieve your vision.

**How do I use it?**
Print out the template – A3 if you can

Get yourself in to a positive environment and a relaxed frame of mind.

Reflect on the questions in the template and jot down what comes up.

Read, reflect and re-do as necessary.

Revisit after a good night's sleep and see what else comes up.

Then take massive action!

Review and adapt regularly.

# GAME PLAN

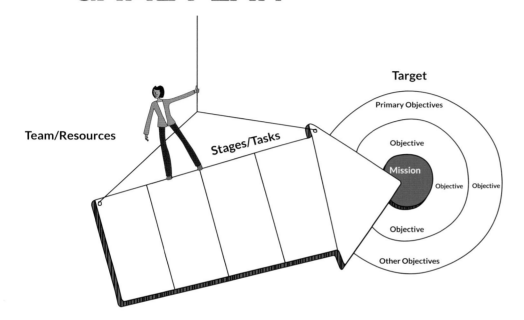

**Target**

Primary Objectives

Objective

Mission

Objective   Objective

Objective

Other Objectives

Team/Resources

Stages/Tasks

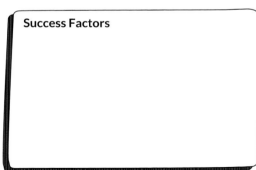

**Success Factors**

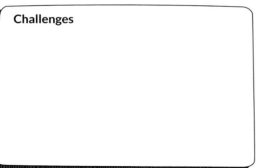

**Challenges**

## What is it?

Dave Sibbert and his team have created many fantastic templates you can use to great effect for collaborative planning. Go check them out. I have used them many times with great results.

## How do I use it?

Allow two to three hours for this activity.

You will need a large sheet of paper with the plan outline drawn on it – preferably A1 or larger and a quantity of marker pens.

- Start with the target area of the plan; clarify the project goal and the specific outcomes and deliverables for the project or activity.
- Then look at the project team, or resources and assess what you have in terms of people, their skills, resources etc.
- For the tasks/project plan area of the plan you will need to ensure the right sequence. Try to keep it top level.
- For the success factors, think about what good will look like when you achieve the goal as well as the shared behaviours and principles that you believe will assist you in being successful.
- Finally identify challenges and kill any risks.

# VISION BOARD

**What is it?**
A visual way to express your vision of the future.

**How do I use it?**
Get yourself in a positive and resourceful mindset.

Get into a stimulating environment for you.

Pick a template or create your own. Canva have templates you can download. Brainstorm what you want to achieve from life. Find some pictures and words that best describe your vision. (www.canva.com)

Get creative and create a board that makes the hairs on the back of your neck stand up and fills your heart full of joy!

# VISION IT

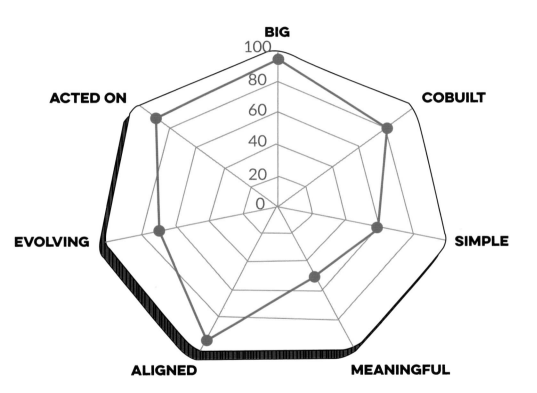

## What is it?

A tool to ensure you create a compelling vision.
It provides all the elements you need to included and helps you to check it by using a scoring chart.

## How do I use it?

- **BIG** A powerful vision is bold and exciting. It should make the hairs on the back of your neck stand up. You need to think big!
- **COBUILT** A good vision should be built by the people who are going to live it. Inclusion = Commitment
- **SIMPLE** A powerful vision must be easy to understand and be able to be remembered on a day to day basis.
- **MEANINGFUL** A good vision is understood by everyone in the organisation who can articulate it with meaning and show how they contribute.
- **ALIGNED** A good vision is useless unless there are aligned strategies and plans in place to achieve it. Everything must be focused in the same direction and momentum created in achieving the vision.
- **EVOLVING** A good vision must evolve as opportunities arrive and conditions change.
- **ACTED ON** For a vision to realise results, people throughout the organisation must act on it and use it as a guiding framework for decision making.

# 5 STRENGTHS QUESTIONS

**What is it?**

A strength is an activity that makes a person feel strong. It's an activity that strengthens them. This tool helps you find out what invigorates your team, what demotivates them and where their aspirations lie. This information is valuable and will help you identify the areas to enhance their performance. The five questions are designed to be used in coaching sessions or team review sessions to ensure strengths are being used.

**How do I use it?**

1. Create a safe and trusting climate.
2. Ask the five questions and listen.
3. Explore the answers and question more to expand.
4. Create actions.
5. Carry out ongoing support and review often.

**1.**

**What was your best day at work in the last three months?**

What were you doing?
Why did you love it?
How can we repeat it?

**2.**

**What was your worst day at work in the last three months?**

What were you doing?
Why did it drain you?
How can we avoid it?

**3.**

**What is the best manager relationship you've ever had?**

What made it so good?

**4.**

**What's the best recognition you've ever had?**

What made it so good?

**5.**

**When in your career have you learnt most?**

What was happening?
How were you learning?

# PERMA

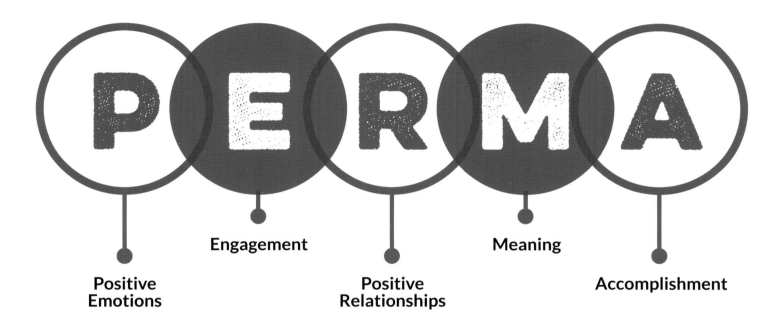

Engagement

Positive
Emotions

Positive
Relationships

Meaning

Accomplishment

**What is it?**

Martin Seligman, one of the founders of positive psychology, developed a five-core element model of psychological well-being and happiness. Seligman believes that these five elements can help people work towards a life of fulfilment, happiness, and meaning.

**How do I use it?**

Ask yourself these questions and generate your solutions in the form of actions you will take.

- How do we create positivity and great feelings?
- How do we ensure we are fully engaged?
- How do we improve relationships?
- How do we promote purpose and meaning?
- How do we reward and celebrate successes?

# WHEEL OF LIFE

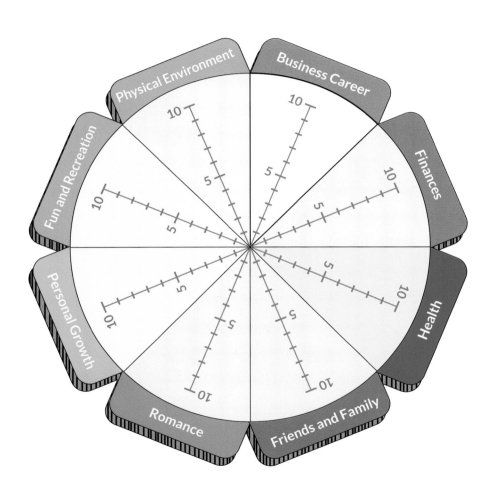

## What is it?

A tool to explore your current life situation. It quickly identifies areas of imbalance and helps you to create goals and set priorities based on your life vision. This means to know what you want in life, and I mean really know. What makes your heart sing? What gets you bouncing out of bed in the morning? What gives you energy? What are you working towards?

## How do I use it?

- For each segment ask yourself, "On a scale from 1-10 (with 10 being the ideal), how satisfied am I with this area of my life?" Don't over-think it, just 'go with your gut'.
- Rate each segment until you have a second 'inner' wheel. Ask, "If I had to travel far with these wheels, how would the ride be?"
- Choose the segment you feel to be most out of balance.
- Consider all the small successes that make up this score i.e., "What is working well?"
- If anything were possible, what would your ideal satisfaction score be? This is your life vision for one area of your life.
- Compare your 2 lists: 'What I have' and 'What I Want'. What do you notice?
- Take a moment to 'live' your ideal score for this segment; Feel what it is like, visualise your ideal day, week, month, year. The more detail, the better!
- What could you do to move up one point between your score today and your ideal?
- Decide on an achievable action step to bring you one step closer to your target.

# BUSINESS MODEL YOU

WHO HELPS YOU
## WHAT YOU DO
HOW YOU HELP
### HOW YOU INTERACT
## WHO YOU HELP
### WHO YOU ARE & WHAT YOU HAVE
### HOW THEY KNOW YOU & HOW YOU DELIVER
## WHAT YOU GIVE
## WHAT YOU GET

## What is it?

Tim Clark innovated the Business Model Canvas to make it useful for planning complex career decisions.

The Business Model You helps with complex quandaries when the user wishes to make changes to their career.

It does so by focusing on a person's talents, goals, needs, desires, and environment. Like the Business Model Canvas, the Business Model You also consists of nine valuable elements.

## How do I use it?

- Download the canvas from businessmodelyou.com
- Fill out the canvas and reflect on your personal environment.
- Talk to people who know you well, family and friends.
- Reflect and fill out a few times to ensure you have it right.
- Then agree actions.

**www.businessmodelyou.com**

# PILLAR TWO:
# VITALITY

**LEADERSHIP BRAND**
**DIET**
**SLEEP**
**MOVEMENT**
**MINDFULNESS**
**BRAIN GYM**
**YOGA**
**PAMPERING**
**MASSAGE**
**NATURE**
**ACUPUNCTURE**

# LEADERSHIP BRAND

| | YOUR ANSWERS |
|---|---|
| **STAGE 1 DISCOVERY**<br>**What was your best day at work in the last three months?**<br>What were you doing? Why did you love it? How can we repeat it? | |
| **What was your worst day at work in the last three months?**<br>What were you doing? Why did it drain you? How can we avoid it? | |
| **What is the best manager relationship you've ever had?**<br>What made it so good? | |
| **What's the best recognition you've ever had?**<br>What made it so good? | |
| **When in your career have you learnt most?**<br>Why? What was happening? How were you learning? | |
| **What are your values and beliefs?**<br>What is important to you? | |
| **Your friends and colleagues thoughts**<br>Once you have done this ask your friends and colleagues what they think your strengths are. | |
| **STAGE 2: FOCUS**<br>**What do you want to be famous for?**<br>Summarise your answers above, what are the patterns, themes? | |
| **STAGE 3: COMMUNICATE**<br>**Create your leadership brand statement**<br>"I want to be known for being _____, and _____<br>so that I can deliver_____" | |
| **STAGE 4: ALIGN**<br>**Take massive action:**<br>What are you going to stop, start and continue doing to live your brand? | |

# DIET

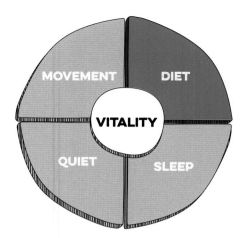

There has been plenty words written on diet, we are bombarded with recommendations and photo shopped pictures to get us to buy into the latest fads, pills and potions.

My personal view is to see food as fuel for your body and mind. What you put in you get out. Eat the best food you can afford and cut out as much processed food as you can.

It's a great idea to work with a qualified nutrionalist to find out what works best for you and create a healthy diet.

Make eating enjoyable and something you do in a relaxed and enjoyable way. Try not to rush eating, eat on the go, or eat at your desk or cut meals out because you are too busy. Remember food is a key part to your health and happiness.

At the end of the day take qualified advice, find what works for you and most of all enjoy it. Eating should be a pleasure and feel like it's rebuilding your energy.

Remember to ensure you remain hydrated by drinking enough water too! One of the triggers of feeling hungry is when you are dehydrated!

**Five diets you could explore that have proven science behind them are:**
1. Low carb, whole food diet - vegetables, meat, fish, eggs, fruits, nuts, and good fats
2. Mediterranean diet - plenty of vegetables, fruits, fish, poultry, whole grains, legumes, dairy products, and extra virgin olive oil
3. Paleo diet – focused on unprocessed food
4. Vegan diet – based exclusively on plant foods
5. Gluten free diet – whole foods that are gluten free

# SLEEP

**Sleep is such an important part of resiliency. Here are a number of useful tips:**

1. Create a good environment - invest in a good mattress and comfortable pillows. Keep your bedroom clean and tidy and make sure there is plenty of fresh air and the room is not too hot. Remove all electronic devices, including TVs and Computers
2. Get into a relaxing bedtime ritual
3. Put your phone in airplane mode or off
4. Reduce blue light exposure in the evening
5. Relaxing music can help
6. Set yourself up for sleep – reduce alcohol and caffeine – wind down
7. Exercise helps to remove stress and relax the body – but not too late in the evening
8. Intimacy is wonderful!
9. Avoid heavy meals in the evening
10. Avoid bright lights in the evening – get plenty of sunlight during the day though!
11. Get the best blackout curtains you can afford
12. Try to sleep and wake at consistent times
13. Take a melatonin supplement. Lavender, magnesium and other supplements can help too. Check with a nutrionalist first.
14. Take a relaxing bath or shower
15. Try not to drink any fluids 1-2 hours before going to bed

# QUIET

Mindfulness is a great practice to boost your vitality and resilience.

Mindfulness meditation involves sitting silently and paying attention to thoughts, sounds, the sensations of breathing or parts of the body, bringing your attention back whenever the mind starts to wander. When we practice mindfulness, we're practicing the art of creating space for ourselves—space to think, space to breathe, space between ourselves and our reactions.

While mindfulness might seem simple, it's not necessarily all that easy. The real work is to make time every day to just keep doing it.

**Here's a short practice to get you started:**
- Take a seat. Find a place to sit that feels calm and quiet to you.
- Set a time limit. If you're just beginning, it can help to choose a shorter time, such as 5 or 10 minutes.
- Notice your body. You can sit in a chair with your feet on the floor, you can sit loosely cross-legged, in lotus posture, you can kneel—all are fine. Just make sure you are stable and in a position you can stay in for a while.
- Feel your breath. Follow the sensation of your breath as it goes out and as it goes in.
- Notice when your mind has wandered. Inevitably, your attention will leave the sensations of the breath and wander to other places. When you get around to noticing this—in a few seconds, a minute, five minutes—simply return your attention to the breath.
- Be kind to your wandering mind. Don't judge yourself or obsess over the content of the thoughts you find yourself lost in. Just come back.

- That's it! That's the practice. You go away, you come back, and you try to do it as kindly as possible.
- Headspace is a great place to go and explore mindfulness. There are plenty of other great apps out there too.

**www.headspace.com/mindfulness**

# MOVEMENT

Getting the body moving throughout the day is important to relieve stress, reduce anxiety and boost vitality.

We need three main types of exercise for optimal health: aerobic, strength training, and stretching.

We recommend finding a qualified and holistic coach to support you.

**The three main types of exercise we need are:**

1. Aerobic exercise works the cardiovascular system (lungs, blood vessels, heart muscle) and increases the efficiency of aerobic muscle fibre. It helps lower blood pressure, oxygenates the whole body, including the brain, uses calories, and helps prevent cardiovascular disease.

2. Strength building exercise works on the muscle fibres, bones, and cartilage and builds anaerobic muscle fibre. It increases the metabolic rate, increases vitality, increases efficient glucose utilization for diabetes prevention, increases bone density, prevents arthritis, improves balance, and reverses declining strength that comes from inactivity.

3. Stretching increases flexibility, coordination, balance, and agility and improves free movement. If you avoid stretching muscles shorten and joint tissue weakens, causing stiffness with aging. Stretching improves arthritis pain and helps prevent injuries.

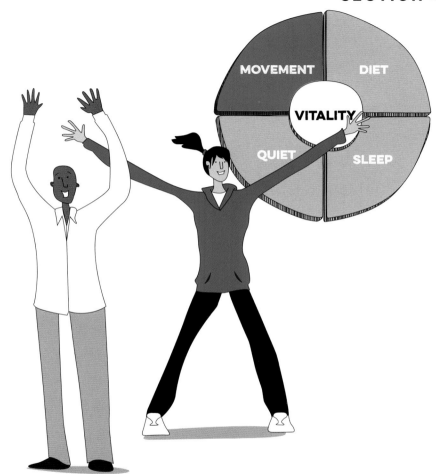

Find exercise you enjoy and make it a habit. Make sure you don't over do it and ensure you build in enough time to recover based on your fitness levels. Don't ever compare yourself to others. Focus on you!

# BRAIN GYM

Brain Gym® is an educational, movement based programme which uses simple movements to integrate the whole brain, senses and body, preparing the person with the physical skills they need to learn effectively. Brain Gym can be used to improve a wide range of learning, attention and behaviour skills.

Although used extensively in schools, we can use it as adults too!

**The benefits are:**
• Helps you get sharper and smarter
• Boosts self-esteem and confidence levels
• Improves health and boosts the immunity and healing
• Improves eyesight
• Improves creativity
• Boosts communicative skills

Now that can't be a bad thing.

It consists of 26 simple and pleasant movements aiming at improving learning skills through the use of both brain hemispheres.

**Exercises include:**
• cross-crawl • sit-up cross crawl • think of an 'X' • lazy 8s • alphabet 8s • the elephant • double doodle • neck rolls • the owl • the rocker • belly breathing • the energizer • arm activation • foot flex • calf pump • gravity glider • the grounder • water • brain buttons • earth buttons • balance buttons • space buttons • energy yawn • thinking cap • hook-ups • positive points

Check out https://braingym.org.uk/ for more information on the exercises. There are plenty of videos on YouTube showing the exercises. Don't be put off by the fact it was designed for children. We can all benefit. Many of the exercises are used in elite sport warm up routines!

# YOGA

Yoga is an ancient form of exercise that focuses on strength, flexibility and breathing to boost physical and mental wellbeing. The main components of yoga are postures (a series of movements designed to increase strength and flexibility) and breathing.

The practice originated in India about 5,000 years ago and has been adapted in other countries in a variety of ways. Yoga is now commonplace in leisure centres, health clubs, schools, hospitals and surgeries.

What are the health benefits of yoga?
Dozens of scientific trials of varying quality have been published on yoga.

While there's scope for more rigorous studies on its health benefits, most studies suggest yoga is a safe and effective way to increase physical activity, especially strength, flexibility and balance.

There's some evidence that regular yoga practice is beneficial for people with high blood pressure, heart disease, aches and pains – including lower back pain – depression and stress.

There are many different styles of yoga, such as Ashtanga, Iyengar and Sivananda. Some styles are more vigorous than others, while some may have a different area of emphasis, such as posture or breathing. Many yoga teachers develop their own practice by studying more than one style.

No style is necessarily better or more authentic than any other. The key is to choose a class appropriate for your fitness level.

**The main UK yoga associations are:**
British Wheel of Yoga (BWY), the Sport England-recognised governing body for yoga
Independent Yoga Network
Iyengar Yoga (UK)
Yoga Alliance Professionals

# PAMPERING

**The benefits are great:**
1. Helps to de-stress
2. Helps with anti-ageing
3. Promotes a better sleep
4. Relieves aches and pains
5. Supports weight loss
6. Improved blood flow and circulation
7. Preventing varicose veins
8. Increased happiness
9. Reduced frequency of headaches
10. Promotes radiant skin
11. Disconnect
12. Breathe easy

The word spa is widely believed to mean "health through water". Spa can also be defined as a treatment involving healing waters and it includes several different massage therapies. Through these massages, spa centres offer a relaxing atmosphere for physical and mental tranquillity.

Promising wellness and prettiness through the healing power of water, spa treatments date back all the way to the Roman era. It is known that the Romans built baths for soldiers returning home from war to help relieve symptoms of fatigue and exhaustion.

Let's face it we can all do with a good pamper from time to time, even if we are a warrior! There's nothing more luxurious and relaxing than a trip to the spa. Experiencing a massage after a stressful time, or treating yourself to a facial before a big event. Spa treatments are a luxury that many of us love to indulge in.

# MASSAGE

Massage is perhaps one of the oldest healing traditions. Many ancient peoples – including the Ancient Greeks, Egyptians, Chinese and Indians – were convinced of the therapeutic properties of massage and used it to treat a variety of ailments.

Massage therapy is the practice of kneading or manipulating a person's muscles and other soft-tissue in order to improve their wellbeing or health. It is a form of manual therapy that includes holding, moving, and applying pressure to the muscles, tendons, ligaments and fascia.

The term 'massage therapy' is used to describe a wide variety of techniques that vary in the manner in which touch, pressure and the intensity of the treatment is applied.

**Research indicates that massage and myotherapy are effective in managing:**
subacute/chronic low back pain
delayed onset muscle soreness (DOMS)
anxiety
stress
soft tissue injuries
high blood pressure
insomnia.

**They can also be effectively used to support people with:**
a chronic disease
a life threatening illness such as cancer.

# NATURE

One study, conducted by scientists in Japan, monitored the effects of a practice known as "Shinrin-yoku," which literally means forest-bathing. The study involved field experiments in 24 forests across Japan, with 280 participants in total. In each experiment, the scientists would send one half of the participants into the woods, and the other half into a city. The next day, those who spent time in the woods would be sent into a city and vice versa. At the end of it all, the scientists found those who spent their day in forests had "lower concentrations of cortisol, lower pulse rate and lower blood pressure."

Spending time in green space or bringing nature into your everyday life can benefit both your mental and physical wellbeing. For example, doing things like growing food or flowers, exercising outdoors or being around animals can have lots of positive effects. It can:

- improve your mood
- reduce feelings of stress or anger
- help you take time out and feel more relaxed
- improve your physical health
- improve your confidence and self esteem
- help to be more active
- help you make new connections
- provide peer support

Shinrin-Yoku is becoming a cornerstone of preventive health care and healing in Japanese medicine. Here's how you can benefit from it:

**Step 1** – Leave behind your phone, camera or any other distractions, so that you can be fully present in the experience.

**Step 2** – Leave behind your goals and expectations. Wander aimlessly, allowing your body to take you wherever it wants.

**Step 3** – Pause from time to time, to look more closely at a leaf or notice the sensation of the path beneath your feet, notice the different smells and feelings you are producing.

**Step 4** – Find a comfy spot to take a seat and listen to the sounds around you. See how the behaviour of the birds and other animals changes when they become used to your presence.

**Step 5** – If you go with others, make an agreement to resist talking until the end of the walk, when you could gather to share your experiences.

This also works in other environments such as the beach, mountains, lakes, rivers and even being outside in towns and cities. The key is to get outside regularly. Our schools had it right when they sent us outside every 45 minutes to play!

# ACUPUNCTURE

Acupuncture is a treatment derived from ancient Chinese medicine. Fine needles are inserted at certain sites in the body for therapeutic or preventative purposes. Traditional acupuncture is based on the belief that an energy, or "life force", flows through the body in channels called meridians. This life force is known as Qi (pronounced "chee").

Practitioners who use acupuncture in the traditional way believe that when Qi does not flow freely through the body, this can cause illness. They also believe acupuncture can restore the flow of Qi, and so restore health.

Acupuncture involves the insertion of very thin needles through your skin at strategic points on your body. A key component of traditional Chinese medicine, acupuncture is most commonly used to treat pain.

Increasingly, it is being used for overall wellness, including stress management.

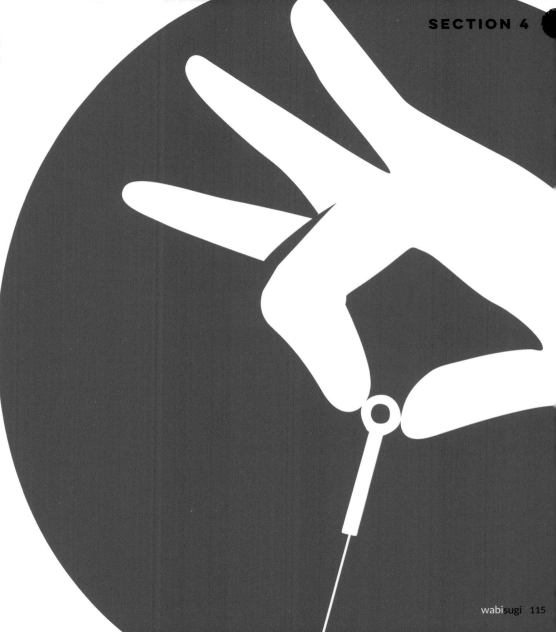

# PILLAR THREE:
# SUPPORT

**6Ps**
**FLOWS**
**NETWORKING SKILLS**
**MASTERMINDING**
**HIGH CHALLENGE/**
**SUPPORT**
**TRUST BEHAVIOURS**
**VIRTUAL SUPPORT**
**GROUPS**
**FAMILY AND FRIENDS**

# 6Ps TEAM CANVAS

Building a team around you is key to boosting your resilience. What can be very draining is doing tasks that you aren't very good at and don't fit your personality. The key is to use your strengths and build a team of complimentary skills. The key to what we call, playing to position.

Creating a team is all about creating a common purpose, building trust and gaining clarity about what needs to be done and how you should do it. Creating a 6Ps Team Canvas can start you on that journey. It keeps the team focused and provides a reference point to remind everyone what was agreed, keeping priorities in everyone's mind.

To create and build your team, recruit people with all the skill sets you need and then get together to use the 6Ps template, ensure everyone involved has sight of the template (can be done remotely if needed).

Ask each question in turn. To enable everyone to contribute, ask them to write down their thoughts on post-it notes as individuals first and stick onto flip chart paper or a wall etc., somewhere visible for everyone.

Identify any common threads and group these post-its. Note in the relevant box on the template. At this stage you may need a page per box in the template. Once all questions have been answered bring together the team's thoughts into one place, for example, typing up a 6Ps page, which shows the teams commitments for each of the areas. A credit card sized version could be produced for everyone to keep at hand. Send out to everyone involved. Refer to this regularly at meetings etc., to keep it fresh and alive. It can be updated if necessary to keep it relevant.

| | |
|---|---|
| **PURPOSE:**<br>Why are we here? What difference are we making? | |
| **PEOPLE:**<br>Who's on the team and their roles and responsibilities?<br>What do we each need to be at our best?<br>What do we need to be careful of?<br>What are some of the obstacles we need to be aware of?<br>What skills and attributes do we have that we need to utilise? | |
| **PERFORMANCE:**<br>How do we know we are a successful as a team?<br>What are the Key Success Factors | |
| **PRINCIPLES:**<br>What are our guiding principles?<br>What do we stand for?<br>Team values?<br>What is important to do on this project? | |
| **PROCESSES:**<br>What are our ways of getting together, types of meeting, routines, decision making, team processes?<br>How do we execute and evaluate? | |
| **PRIDE:**<br>What do we want to be famous for? How do we want to be described by others? Team brand? | |

# FLOWS

FLOWS is a framework that identifies what needs to be in place to create a positive team climate.

When leading your team, review your leadership behaviours and ensure you focus on all 5 areas. Is your team focused, are they learning, do they have the opportunity to perform, do they feel valued and are they supported?

Early on in the team formation it's a great idea to generate ideas with the team in a workshop. Set up an effective environment to generate ideas and then get the team to think about what actions you can do for each element and create a plan.

Use the framework on a regular basis to review performance.

| Enabling Element | Actions I will do.... |
|---|---|
| **FOCUS**<br>Ensuring your teams have a clear understanding of business goals and direction, why they are important, and how they contribute to achievement | |
| **LEARNING**<br>Ensuring teams and individuals take opportunities to grow and develop through training and self-development, and take responsibility for sharing work based learning with others | |
| **OPPORTUNITY**<br>Ensuring that teams are able to utilise the full expertise and capability of every team member, and have the autonomy to do so | |
| **WORTH**<br>Ensuring teams are widely recognised for their capability and achievement, praised and thanked for their efforts and results, and appropriately rewarded for their contribution | |
| **SUPPORT**<br>Ensuring that every team feels it has the resources, information and management support and commitment it needs to be able to perform at the highest level | |

# NETWORKING

Networking can be a bit like marmite, it's a love-hate thing! Networking is the process of meeting new people who can be useful to you in your life, often through social activities. One thing is for sure though is that building a strong network around you will boost your resiliency.

Having a rich resource of people, who you have a relationship with and have a variety of skillsets, is useful when solving challenges and decision making.

Here's four tips identified in an HBR article - Learn To Love Networking by Tiziana Casciaro, Francesca Gino and Maryam Kouchaki.

**Focus on learning –**
It's a good idea to view networking as a process of boosting your learning. Think of it as learning with and from others. Building a network of people with different backgrounds will increase your access to knowledge and ideas.

**Identify common interests –**
The next step in making networking more palatable, is to think about how your interests and goals align with those of people you meet and how that can help you forge meaningful working relationships.

**Think Broadly About What You Can Give**
Even when you do not share an interest with someone, you can probably find something valuable to offer by thinking beyond the obvious.

**Find a Higher Purpose**
Another factor that affects people's interest in and effectiveness at networking is the primary purpose they have in mind when they do it. Find a common purpose and you'll find it more rewarding.

# MASTERMINDING

Mastermind groups offer a combination of problem-solving, brainstorming, education, mentoring, peer accountability and support in a group setting.

A mastermind group helps you and your mastermind group members achieve success. Members challenge each other to set strong goals, and more importantly, to accomplish them.

Napoleon Hill explained it clearly and encouraged people to gather together in a structured, repeatable environment for the success of all. Napoleon Hill wrote about the mastermind group principle as:

"The coordination of knowledge and effort of two or more people, who work toward a definite purpose, in the spirit of harmony.

No two minds ever come together without thereby creating a third, invisible, intangible force, which may be likened to a third mind [the master mind]."
www.naphill.org

## The Process

- A member of the group will volunteer a challenge/issue/question to start the discussion.

- The group will have 3 minutes to ask context building questions to help understand the owner's challenge.

- At the end of the 3 minutes the owner of the question must move out of the group and sit in a chair with his/her back to the group. A notepad and pen will be useful at this point.

- The remainder of the group now have 10 minutes to discuss how they may already have or would answer the question.

- During the 10 minutes, the owner of the question cannot contribute to the discussion.

- At the end of the 10 minutes, the owner will turn around and share either two things they will do as a result of the discussion or the two things that resonate with them the most.

# HIGH CHALLENGE/HIGH SUPPORT CULTURE

As a leader it is important to create a high performance culture where success is inevitable.

A high performance culture is one where you initiate high challenge AND high support.

The model shows what happens if you don't do both elements at a high level.

If high support and low challenge it's too comfortable. You won't get the best performance possible.

If you create a low support and low challenge culture, you get apathy and very low performance.

If high challenge and low support you create high stress and burnout. High performance is not sustainable, you may get some early wins but then performance drops off and you get into what we call the dead body syndrome. This is where you get 'attendees' just surviving!

Make sure you create a challenging culture with plenty of support.

Then it's really exciting, rewarding and people will surprise you with what they achieve.

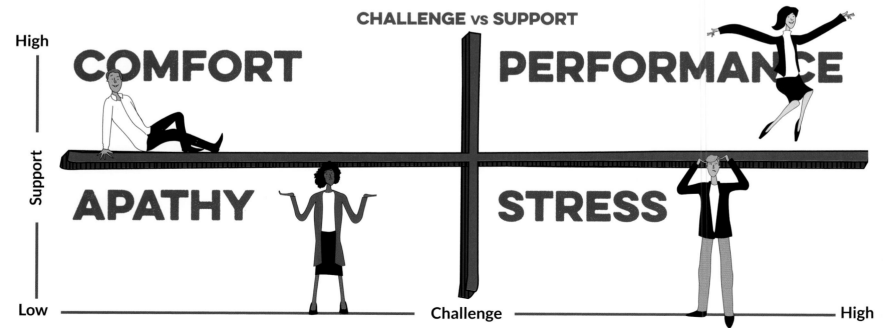

**CHALLENGE vs SUPPORT**

High — COMFORT    PERFORMANCE

Support

APATHY    STRESS

Low —    Challenge    High

# TRUST BEHAVIOURS

Building trusting relationships is a great way to boost the support you need for outstanding resiliency. In his book The Speed of Trust, Stephen M.R. Covey identified 13 behaviours that will build trust.

**13.** Extend Trust

**12.** Keep Commitments

**11.** Listen First

**10.** Practice Accountablilty

**9.** Clarify Expectations

**8.** Confront Reality

**7.** Get Better

**6.** Deliver Results

**5.** Show Loyalty

**4.** Right Wrongs

**3.** Create Transparency

**2.** Demonstrate Respect

**1.** Talk Straight

## "THE FIRST JOB OF A LEADER IS TO INSPIRE TRUST"

STEPHEN M. R. COVEY

# SUPPORT GROUPS

Support groups take networking a step further and build strong relationships to support each other. These are people you can rely on to have your back.

They are usually peer groups. They can be volunteer groups set up to help with things like mental heath or abuse.

A support group provides an opportunity for people to share personal experiences and feelings, coping strategies, or first-hand information about diseases or treatments.

Usually face to face, they can be virtual as well. Support and self-help groups address many issues. Common ones include:

Chronic illnesses/conditions—such as cancer, diabetes, fibromyalgia, post traumatic stress disorder, alcoholism, and depression.

Situational crises—such as divorce, unemployment, single parenting, widowhood, care giving, and surviving a loved one's suicide.

Personal growth and wellness—such as weight loss, smoking cessation, exercise, men's and women's groups.

Family support—which includes groups that help family members cope with a loved one's illness or condition.

Depending on your situation you can explore and join the relevant support group to ensure you boost your resilience and bounce-back ability.

As they say, a problem shared is a problem halved!

# FAMILY AND FRIENDS

The final area of support you can get can be from family and friends. Depending on the background, context, situation and history, family and friends can be a great source of inspiration and support.

The family and close friend bond can be strong and a powerful way to gain the support you need.

It includes grandparents, older siblings, aunts and uncles and family friends, and god parents. They could be anybody who is a relative or already knows you well and has an intent to support you.

Creating a strong team around you is an effective way to create a lovely protective bubble. Knowing you can trust and rely on people around you gives you a sense of invincibility. Knowing there is someone who you can talk to and/or will support you is a wonderful feeling.

After all, as human beings we are tribal and need that sense of team.

# PILLAR FOUR:
# COMPOSURE

**EMOTIONAL INTELLIGENCE**
**TRIGGER AWARENESS**
**STRENGTHS**
**RED 2 BLUE**
**BREATHING**
**REFRAMING**
**EFT – TAPPING**
**NAMING**
**ANCHORING**

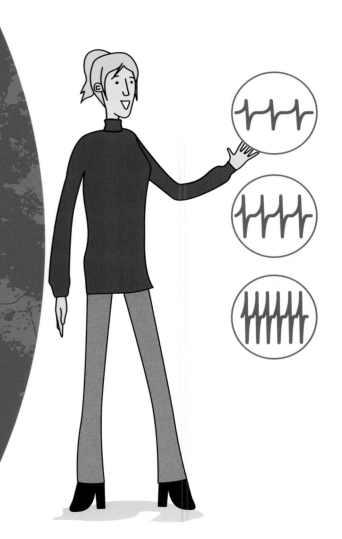

# EMOTIONAL INTELLIGENCE

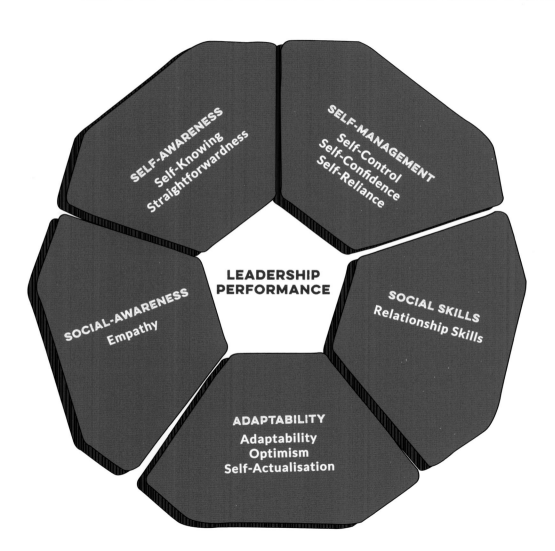

**What is it?**
A framework that indicates the key elements required to become more emotionally intelligent.

**How do I use it?**
**Self Awareness:** The ability to know one's emotions, strengths, weaknesses, drivers, values and goals and recognise how they impact on others while using gut feelings to guide decisions.

**Self Management:** Involves controlling or redirecting one's disruptive emotions and impulses and adapting to changing circumstances.

**Social Skills:** Managing relationships to move people in the desired direction.

**Adaptability:** Willingness to change approach to drive desired outcomes, to re-prioritise when business needs arise.

**Social Awareness:** Empathy, considering other people's feelings especially when making decisions.

# TRIGGER AWARENESS

Understanding what triggers you is all part of developing your emotional intelligence and resilience. If you are self aware of what triggers you, it's easier to understand and choose to make a different response.

Remember, there is a big gap between stimulus and response which is called your point of choice. Being mentally tough is your ability to choose a positive response regardless to the stimulus.

It's not easy, but with practice (and sometimes help from a qualified practitioner) we can overcome our experiences that have caused our triggers.

The starting point is to use the checklist to start the process of identifying your triggers.

CBT, Tapping and Belief Work can help. If you have deep trauma or blocks then professional help is required. We are happy to recommend suitable people if required.

Use the sheet to identify your triggers and explore why these are triggers. Be more aware of them in your everyday interactions. Catching them early is a great way to let them go, save energy and be more resilient.

Remember it's not the situation you're in, or the other person making you feel like you do, it's your choice of how you respond to the stimulus. How empowering is that!

- Being Told No
- Waiting
- Hunger
- Cheating
- Being Touched
- Too Much To Do
- Rumours or Gossip
- Hurt or Pain
- Being Scared
- Bad News

- Unfair Treatment
- Tests and Grades
- Being Late
- Being Criticized
- Being Tired
- Being Ignored
- A Misunderstanding
- Being Disrespected
- Being Bumped Into
- Loud Noises

- Losing a Game
- An Accident
- Being Left Out
- Being Bullied
- An Interruption
- Things Do Not Go as Planned
- Things Are Not Fair
- Not Understanding What To Do
- Being Told What To Do

# MARSHALLING STRENGTHS

We've talked about identifying your strengths and ensuring you are playing to your strengths.

Once you've identified them, it's all about making sure you use them effectively and building a team around you to support any weaknesses.

The key is not to try and change yourself but to play to your natural and easier ways of working. Trying to play to your weaknesses can be draining. Playing to your strengths gives you energy – useful when it comes to resilience!

Here's a way to ensure you do that effectively…

| **Understand your strengths…** | **Harness strengths to goals** | **Use your strengths to compensate** | **Combine strengths for multiplier** | **Calibrate: don't overplay strengths** |
|---|---|---|---|---|
| In your situation and context What do you do well and love to do? What results do you achieve by using these strengths? | Be clear about what you want to achieve. Work out which strengths will be most effective in helping you achieve your goals. | For the areas where you might struggle (risk), what strength do you have which can compensate and help overcome that risk? | Get your strengths working together to maximise impact. We all have different strengths, so the combinations and affect will be different. | Watch out that you don't take a strength too far. Use it as much as appropriate for your context and situation. Dial it up and down according to need. |

**Monitor and Refine**
As you use your strengths, reflect and refine what you are doing. What's working?  What isn't?  What could be better?
Refine your actions based on your learning.

# RED2BLUE

Red 2 Blue is a philosophy used by elite sport to operate at the highest levels.

It's about controlling your physiology when it really matters.

Many of the techniques we have shared with you, like heart breathing will help.

If you want to learn more about how it's used in sport and elite military situations, or become a certified coach, head over to Gazing Performance Systems.

Red Head and Blue Head are great metaphors to recognise where you are at any moment and either change from red head or maintain blue head.

### Red Head
Tight and Inhibited
**Desperate**
Results Oriented
## Anxious and Aggressive
Over Compensating

### Blue Head
Loose and Expressive
**In the Moment**
Accurate and On Task
## Calm and Clear

# HEART BREATHING

Heart-focused breathing is about directing your attention to the heart area and breathing a little more deeply than normal.

As you breathe in, imagine you are doing so through your heart, and, as you breathe out, imagine it is through your heart. (In the beginning, placing your hand over your heart as you breathe can help you in directing your focus to your heart.)

Typically, HeartMath recommends that you breathe in for about 5 to 6 seconds and breathe out for 5 to 6 seconds. Be sure your breathing is smooth, unforced and comfortable. Although this is not difficult to do, it may take a little time to become used to it, but eventually you will establish your own natural rhythm.

Heart-focused breathing won't take a lot of time out of your day, but it can add lots of benefits to your life. Many people find that heart-focused breathing is an excellent way to start and finish their day, but there are times in between when it is especially beneficial. Try it during a break on the job, at school or while working around the house.

There is no more important time for a few minutes of heart-focused breathing than when you feel your stress buttons being pushed.

These vary from one person to the next, but some you may be familiar with, such as a late bus, train or even plane commute to work; a presentation, important meeting or performance review in the workplace; a big test at school; or a dreaded encounter with someone you'd rather avoid.

https://www.heartmath.org/resources/heartmath-tools/

# REFRAMING

## What is it?

Have you ever seen that "optical illusion" drawing where if you look at it one way it's a pretty lady, and if you look at it another way, it's an old woman?

Which is the "real" or "right" way to look at the picture? Either one is right!

Likewise, there often isn't one "right" way to look at the things that happen in your life. Much of what is "true" about a situation is up to you, and there are typically several equally valid ways to see something.

Reframing helps you see things in a different light.

What we are attempting to do with reframing in a resilience context is to avoid looking at things with negative emotions that lead to dejection, anxiety, and frustration, and instead build a mindset that facilitates positive emotions that work towards resilience and keep you moving forward.

## How do I use it?

So how do you go about changing your beliefs/perspective about something?

## By asking yourself two questions:

1. In what context could this be useful?
2. What else could this mean?

# EFT - TAPPING

People often use EFT tapping when they are feeling anxious or stressed or when they have a specific issue that they would like to resolve. However, it may also be beneficial for a person before an event that they expect to cause stress or anxiety.

**To use EFT tapping, follow these steps:**

**1. Identify the issue**

During this step, the person thinks about the problem that they wish to resolve. They should only choose one issue to focus on at a time.

**2. Test the initial intensity**

A person should rank the intensity of the issue on a scale of 0–10, with 10 being the worst the issue has ever been. This ranking system allows the person to assess the effectiveness of the tapping at the end of the treatment.

**3. The setup**

Before beginning each round of tapping, the person should decide on a simple reminder phrase to repeat while tapping the karate chop point. This point is at the centre of the fleshy part of the outer hand. The reminder phrase should acknowledge the issue and convey self-acceptance in spite of it. For example, a person might choose to say: "Even though I have [issue], I deeply and completely accept myself."

**4. The sequence**

During this step, the individual taps on specific points on the body while repeating the phrase that they have chosen. If a practitioner is performing the treatment, they will carry out the tapping.

**The tapping points, in sequence, are as follows:**

- top of the head **(TOH)** — directly in the centre of the top of the head
- beginning of the eyebrow **(EB)** — the beginning of the brow, just above and to the side of the nose
- side of the eye **(SE)** — on the bone at the outside corner of the eye
- under the eye **(UE)** — on the bone under the eye, approximately 1 inch below the pupil
- under the nose **(UN)** — the point between the nose and upper lip
- chin point **(CH)** — halfway between the underside of the lower lip and the bottom of the chin
- beginning of the collarbone **(CB)** — the point where the breastbone (sternum), collarbone, and first rib intersect
- under the arm **(UA)** — at the side of the body, approximately 4 inches below the armpit

When tapping, use two or more fingertips and repeat the tap approximately five times on each point. While some points — for example, the EB, SE, and UE — have a "twin point" on the other side of the body, it is only necessary to tap on one side. However, individuals can tap these points on both sides if both of their hands are free.

**5. Test the intensity again**

Again, rank the intensity of the issue on a scale of 0–10. Ideally, this will have improved. Repeat the process until the intensity reaches 0 or plateaus.

# NAMING

Apparently there are around 3,000 words to describe emotions in English!

It has been found that having an extensive emotional vocabulary is vital for dealing with challenging feelings to boost your resilience AND increasing the frequency of your positive emotions.

There is a great saying, **name it to tame it.**

Simply naming difficult feelings when you experience them reduces the intensity of your emotional reaction as well as switching on the part of your brain which is responsible for rational thinking. This provides an instant boost for your resilience.

Our brains have a natural negative bias, which means that we need to cultivate and wallow in positive emotions to purposely develop our positivity. Experiencing more positive emotions has a range of huge benefits, including better sleep and increased resilience to adversity.

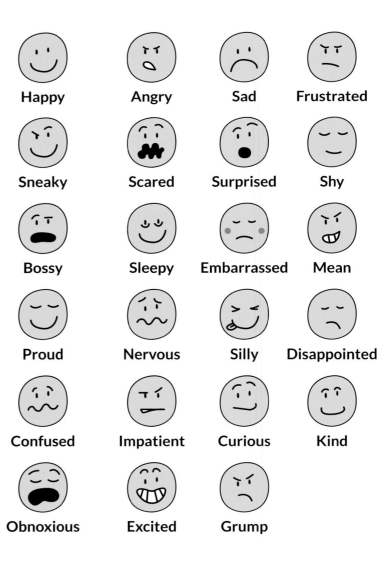

Happy    Angry    Sad    Frustrated

Sneaky    Scared    Surprised    Shy

Bossy    Sleepy    Embarrassed    Mean

Proud    Nervous    Silly    Disappointed

Confused    Impatient    Curious    Kind

Obnoxious    Excited    Grump

# ANCHORING

You've probably heard about Pavlov and how he trained his dogs. Anchoring works the same way and is done by pairing physical touch with a feeling or behaviour you want to have at your disposal. The most common use of anchoring is to have a way to intentionally feel resourceful in the right situations.

For example, you may want to feel more confident when making a presentation. An anchor can grant access to the confidence you have in other situations that are not currently available to you when making presentations.

**Anchoring in 7 Quick and Easy Steps**

1. Determine how you want to feel. In this example let's say more confident.
2. Remember a time when you felt really confident. It can be any memory when you were feeling confident. Relax and let a memory come to mind in which you naturally felt confident.
3. Choose an anchor device that involves touch, such as touching your thumb and forefinger together or making a fist.
4. Remember what you saw, heard and felt in your confident memory. You must put yourself inside the memory as if reliving it. Don't view the memory from a distance, be in it to get the feelings back.
5. Relive the memory until you begin to feel the confidence coming over you in the same way you felt it at the time. As you feel that confidence coming on, activate your anchoring device from step #3.
6. If you chose your thumb and forefinger press when the feeling rises and release when the feeling begins to subside. If you've done this well and there's no underlying reason you shouldn't feel more confident, this anchor is set!
7. Test the anchor by touching your thumb and forefinger together in exactly the same way again and find out if you naturally access that confident state.

If it worked, you now have a confidence anchor! From now on you get to feel confident whenever you touch your thumb and forefinger together.

# PILLAR FIVE:
# PERSISTENCE

**GROWTH MINDSET**
**OPTIMISING**
**CHANGE BRIDGE**
**COACHING CYCLE**
**SCARF**
**JOURNALING**
**SAFE PLACE**

# GROWTH MINDSET

"I can learn to do anything I want to"
"Challenges help me to grow"
**"My effort and attitude determine my abilities"**
"Feedback is constructive"
**"I am inspired by the success of others"**
"I like to try new things"
**"Failure is the limit to my abilities"**

**GROWTH MINDSET**

## "Failure is an opportunity to grow"

A growth mindset is the belief that intelligence can be developed. People with a growth mindset understand they can get smarter through hard work, the use of effective strategies, and help from others when needed. It is contrasted with a fixed mindset: the belief that intelligence is a fixed trait that is set in stone at birth.

Keeping a growth mindset will support the development of your resilience. It's seeing resilience as something you can learn and develop. Just like a muscle, it gets stronger when exercised and recovered in the right way. Using the principles of wabisugi and having a growth mindset will see you achieve extraordinary results.

World-renowned Stanford University psychologist Carol Dweck has written extensively on the subject – it's worth reading her books.

"I am either good at it or not"
"My abilities are unchanging"
**"I don't like to be challenged"**
"My potential is predetermined"
**"When I'm frustrated, I give up"**
"Feedback and criticism are personal"
**"I stick to what I know"**

**FIXED MINDSET**

# OPTIMISING

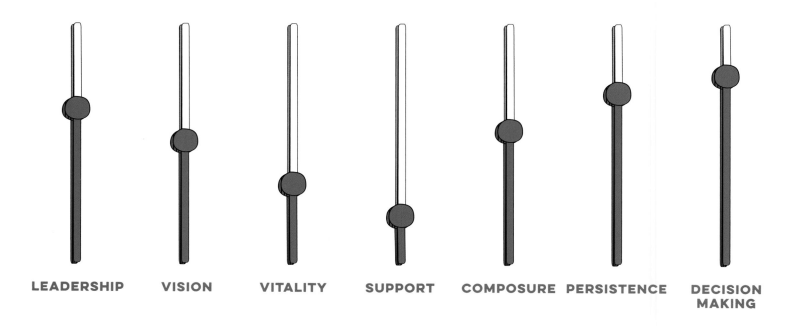

LEADERSHIP VISION VITALITY SUPPORT COMPOSURE PERSISTENCE DECISION MAKING

In this context we talk about optimising as the ability to, understand what is happening, draw down you learning and adjust where your focus is regarding the elements of resilience.

Just like a graphic equalizers used to optimise the different frequencies to get the best sound, optimising lets you focus on the key areas that will get you the best results.

# CHANGE BRIDGE

## What is it?
A visual tool to understand where you are during a piece of change and work out what you can do to move across the bridge.

## How do I use it?
Print out the picture and tune into your thoughts and feelings.

Work out which character best describes how you feel?

Explore what you need to do and what support you need to move across the bridge to the new world!

If struggling use your support network or coach to help you.

It works because you are separating yourself from the problem and using the visual to reframe your next steps.

# COACHING CYCLE

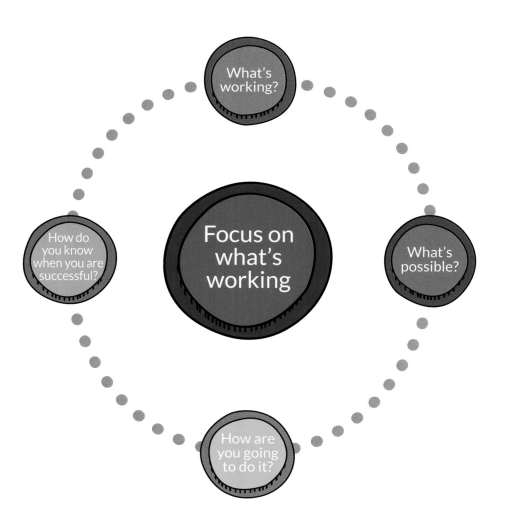

**What's working?**

**Focus on what's working**

**How do you know when you are successful?**

**What's possible?**

**How are you going to do it?**

## What is it?

A tool to build confidence and drive performance improvement. Can be used by a coach on you or you can coach yourself.

## How do I use it?

1. Build self esteem by exploring what went well and what is working.
2. Explore what is possible by building on strengths and what is working. Remember to think big.
3. Build a solution to implement ideas. Determine what support is required.
4. Challenge yourself and check commitment to making it happen. Make sure you know how you will know you are successful.

# SCARF

| | |
|---|---|
| **S** | **STATUS** Relates to how we perceive our position in relation to others we have a relationship with such our boss, peers, direct reports, friends and family. It can include job titles, public and private forms of recognition or criticism, salary and any other aspects associated with status. |
| **C** | **CERTAINTY** Relates to how sure we feel about events/people/situations that affect us. The higher the level of uncertainty, the more likely the threat state will be created. |
| **A** | **AUTONOMY** Relates to the level of control we have over the decisions that affect us. The more autonomous we feel, the more engaged, confident and satisfied we tend to be. |
| **R** | **RELATEDNESS** Concerns the quality of our relationships with others/our sense of belonging. Generally speaking, people like to feel "part of the group". |
| **F** | **FAIRNESS** Relates to our sense of justice and right and wrong. Our perception of whether we have been dealt with fairly can motivate and keep us engaged or it can move us towards a threat state where we are more likely to respond in a defensive way. |

| Element | How important is this to you? | | | How is this being impacted in this situation? | | What are you going to do about it? |
|---|---|---|---|---|---|---|
| **Status** Where you feel you are in the pecking order | 0 | 5 | 10 | Threatened -10 | Rewarded +10 | |
| **Certainty** Your perception of how well you can predict the future | 0 | 5 | 10 | Threatened -10 | Rewarded +10 | |
| **Autonomy** Feeling of having choices, being able to make choices | 0 | 5 | 10 | Threatened -10 | Rewarded +10 | |
| **Relatedness** Feeling safe with other people, trust vs mistrust | 0 | 5 | 10 | Threatened -10 | Rewarded +10 | |
| **Fairness** Feeling of fair connections, fair exchanges | 0 | 5 | 10 | Threatened -10 | Rewarded +10 | |

David Rock has created a great model based on neuroscience and our reactions to change. It helps to build self awareness and understanding to how you are reacting to certain situations.

Using the template go through each of the five elements one at a time.

Score yourself on how important the element is to you, how much you feel threatened or rewarded by the change and what actions you can take to support yourself through the change.

Do this for each element and then create your action plan.

You can also use this in a 121 or team coaching session, virtually or face to face, by asking open questions to guide the conversation through each of the elements.

The key is to build understanding of how you are impacted and then create solutions to move forward.

# JOURNALING

Many famous creatives, writers, innovators and original thinkers use journaling.

The key is just to sit and write whatever comes up. Try not to filter it, just let the pen flow.

Try it first thing in the morning and then review at the end of the day.

Let your mind, heart and gut do the writing.

5 to 10 minutes a day is enough.

If it works for you and is of benefit, try and make it habitual.

Writing, drawing, using mind maps, creating sketches, are all valid. Just let it all come out!

## "IF YOU'RE SERIOUS ABOUT BECOMING A WEALTHY, POWERFUL, SOPHISTICATED, HEALTHY, INFLUENTIAL, CULTURED, AND UNIQUE INDIVIDUAL, KEEP A JOURNAL."

JIM ROHN

Albert Einstein's travel diary to the United States recorded his experiences abroad from November 1930 to June 1931.

(Photo: The Hebrew University of Jerusalem)

# SAFE PLACE

Today's world is a stressful place at times, and it helps to have a few safe spaces where you can be yourself and let your guard down, to relax and replenish your energy.

It's important to have specific times, places, and groups of people who foster a sense of relaxation and emotional safety for you.

It's more difficult to manage the stress of overwhelm, criticism, negativity, and high demands when you're already stressed.

This can help you to build resilience and relieve stress when you need to. Here's how to create "safe spaces" for yourself in different areas of your life.

You could use some of the elements we mentioned in the vitality toolbox such as yoga, nature, gyms, walking, or your home. You could also use some of the methods we shared in the support toolbox such as peer groups, social networks, social media groups, and traditional support groups.

Our personal favourites are a beach or the mountains.

If you are feeling particularly vulnerable there are a number of charities who provide safe places such as
**https://www.safeplaces.org.uk/** and
**https://www.nationalsafeplace.org/**

# PILLAR SIX:
# DECISION MAKING

**5 WHYS**
**CONTEXT MAPPING**
**CAUSE AND EFFECT**
**RADIANT PROBLEM SOLVING**
**KILLING RISK**
**C2E**
**5 SUPER SKILLS**
**DFV ANALYSIS**
**5 QUESTIONS**
**EASE IMPACT GRID**
**WORLD CAFÉ**

# 5 WHYS

Define the probelm:

[                                                            ]

Why is this happening

1. [                              ] Why is that?

2. [                                  ] Why is that?

3. [                                    ] Why is that?

4. [                                      ] Why is that?

5. [                                        ]

## What is it?

The 5 Whys is a simple problem-solving technique that helps you to get to the root of a problem quickly. Made popular in the 1970s by the Toyota Production System, the 5 Whys strategy involves looking at any problem and asking: "Why?" and "What caused this problem?"

Very often, the answer to the first "why" will prompt another "why" and the answer to the second "why" will prompt another and so on; hence the name the 5 Whys strategy.

## Benefits of the 5 Whys include:

- It helps you to quickly determine the root cause of a problem.
- It's simple, and easy to learn and apply.

## How do I use it?

When you're looking to solve a problem, start at the end result and work backward (toward the root cause), continually asking:

"Why?" You'll need to repeat this over and over until the root cause of the problem becomes apparent. Write down the specific problem on a flip chart.

Writing it down helps you formalise the problem and describe it accurately. It also helps a team focus on the same problem. Use brainstorming to ask why the problem occurs then, write the answer down. If this answer doesn't identify the source of the problem, ask 'why?' again and write that answer down.

Loop back to step three until the team agrees that they have identified the problem's root cause. Again, this may take fewer or more than five whys to get to the root cause.

You then need to create a solution to solve the root cause.

# CONTEXT MAPPING

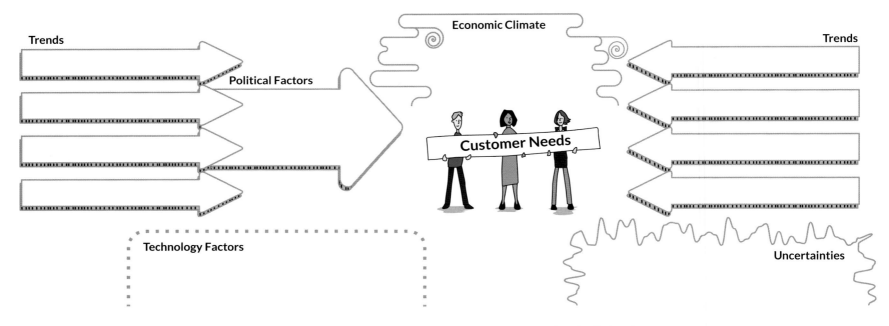

One of the challenges of remaining resilient is that you can easily get overwhelmed with all the changes going on. Context Mapping is a great way to visually understand all the factors impacting on you and get you to calm down and think. The Context Map shown is from the Grove Consulting suit of Graphic Guides we use for strategy work with our clients at Successfactory.

For the purpose of resilience it helps to fully understand your context. Creating a picture of your situation enables you to gain clarity and understanding of what needs to be done. You imagine yourself in the middle of the diagram and then map out all the factors impacting on you. You can change the headings to suit your situation.

Once you have done that you can start to understand your context and then work out what action you need to take to remain resilient and make progress.

# CAUSE AND EFFECT

Cause and effect diagrams can be used to solve problems or create positive outcomes.

**Step 1:** Define problem or outcome and put in the arrowhead.

**Step 2:** Work out the major factors involved and record each as a line coming off the arrow spine.

**Step 3:** Identify possible causes for each of the factors and record on lines coming off the factor line.

You can go a step further and break down each cause to sub causes.

**Step 4:** Analyze diagram and generate actions to overcome problem or achieve outcome.

Remember you can use it to solve a problem and explore what is required to create a positive outcome.

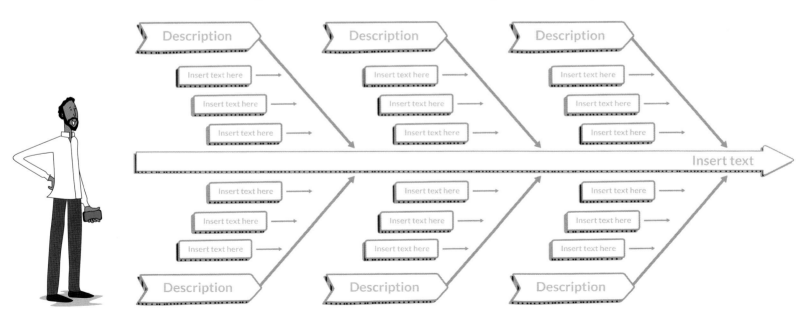

# RADIANT PROBLEM SOLVING

Being able to solve problems quickly is important to remain resilient. Radiant problem solving is a visual collaborative tool to quickly gain ideas of the blockers to achieving a goal and then developing strategies to remove the barriers.

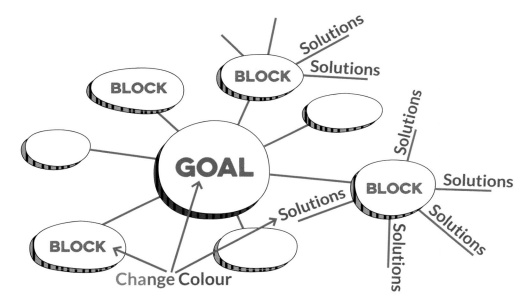

## PROCESS

Decide on your goal, make sure it is phrased as a goal not an issue.
**Group discussion 5 mins**

Brainstorm all the Blocks/ barriers to achieving your goal.
**2 mins**

Take the blocks one at a time and brainstorm all the solutions.
**1 min per block**

Review and reflect on the results, are there common solutions? Can you propose 5 strategies or next steps to work towards the goal?
**5 -15 mins**

# KILLING RISK

Killing risk is an important task to boost your resilience.

Risk taking is good as long as it is well thought through.

Risk management is a process of anticipation and spending enough time foreseeing what could go wrong and making sure you remove the barriers to success in a proactive rather than reactive way.

The process shown is what we have found to work really well for different contexts.

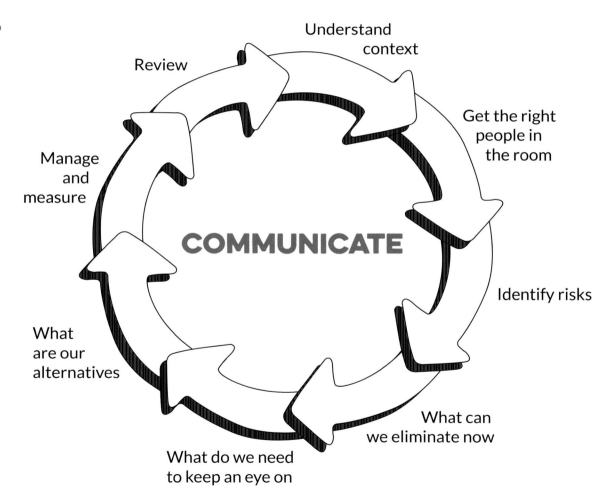

Understand context

Review

Get the right people in the room

Manage and measure

**COMMUNICATE**

Identify risks

What are our alternatives

What can we eliminate now

What do we need to keep an eye on

# COMMUNICATE 2 ENGAGE

One of the key skills for resilient leaders is the ability to communicate in a way that engages people, enables buy-in and inspires action. You need to take people on a journey to enable them to think through what you are asking them to do. The use of stories helps and the more familiar you can make it the better. The more familiar you make it, the less threatening it is. We've found this template a useful way to prepare your message.

**Write it down here how you would describe your idea?**

**It's similar to...**
Description of a popular product/film/brand/person

**But with/without...**
The distinctive properties of your idea

**And what's really great about it is...**
Why they will love it/Why it is of real advantage

# 5 CONVERSATIONAL SUPER SKILLS

| | PRESENCE | HYPER-AWARENESS | DE-CODING | VOICING | FLOW CONTROL |
|---|---|---|---|---|---|
| **PURPOSE** | Be in the moment | Choose your emotion | Seek first to understand | Being courageous | Think beginning, middle and end |
| **WHAT** | Maintaining undivided attention, really "being there" for the other person – by remaining focused on the conversation and able to ignore distractions. | Self-awareness of your biases, beliefs and emotional triggers, meaning you know what is going on for you during a conversation and how to control your emotions. | Drawing out what the other person is really saying by getting to the meaning behind the words so that the other person really feels understood by you. | Expressing your views with courage and conviction in a way that is constructive and helpful for the conversation - even when you have to give tough messages. | Managing conversations – beginning, middle and end - so that it flows well and results in clear outcome that everyone agrees with. |
| **TOP TIPS** | Find a time and space where you can talk without interruptions. **Before the conversation** • Turn off your phone and put it away, and close your laptop • Tune-in to yourself before you start to see if anything is filling your thoughts … if so, consciously 'park' it and decide to come back to it later. Or, if you can't, agree to have the conversation another time **During the conversation** • Pay attention to your attention – check that you are still present. • If your mind wanders, use one of the tips (like your catchphrase). • Paraphrase what the other person is saying to make sure you are correctly hearing what they are telling you. | Take time to understand what 'events' trigger you to respond emotionally during a conversation • Develop your ability to spot when you have been triggered and consciously pause before you act or reply – remember it only takes six seconds for your rational brain to re-engage. • Tune into your physical state – are you feeling hungry, tired, thirsty, hot, cold or stressed? Our physiological state significantly impacts our ability to concentrate and to regulate our emotions. We tend to overlook this, especially when we are busy. • Be curious – if you talk to someone and you find yourself being annoyed or irritated, ask yourself 'why?' – keep learning about yourself. • Make sure you stay aware of your own needs during a conversation. | Checking your mindset when you are listening to someone speak and ask yourself – 'am I listening to understand this person or am I listening so I can just get my view across?'. • Practice listening on three levels: - Listen for Facts – what did they actually say? - Listen for Feelings – what emotions am I picking up? - Listen for Intent – what are they really trying to tell me? • Remember that great conversations start with great questions – so ask more questions and give fewer answers. • Paraphrase what the other person says so you can check you have heard them correctly. • Avoid responding to or judging what other people say until you have understood what they are saying - the 'rush to judge' is one of the quickest ways for conversations to turn into monologues! | If you are worried about having a difficult conversation, remind yourself that you are not alone. So go easy on yourself. • Think logically about the risk of having the conversation versus avoiding it – research shows we tend to focus more on the risk of having the conversation than on the benefits of addressing an issue. • Tune into your feelings and learn to name them – conversations are difficult precisely because they are all about feelings. So before a difficult conversations, write down your feelings • Use the OFT'N model: - Observe – the facts - Feelings – name your emotions - Thoughts – explain your thinking -N- state what you Need. • Rehearse and practice difficult messages – and ask someone you trust to give you feedback • Finally, remember that voicing is about speaking your truth – you have to give other person the opportunity to speak their truth! | **Before the conversation,** ask yourself the following: • What is the objective of the conversation? • What will a successful outcome look like? • What do I want to 'voice'? • How do I feel about this? • What do I think the other person may be thinking or feeling? • How might they react? How will I respond to this? • Where is the best place / time to meet? • How much time will we need **During the conversation** • Agree purpose of the conversation with the other person. • Demonstrate that you are 'present' (Super-Skill one) – and stay present • Honestly 'voice' your feelings (Hyper Awareness and Voicing). • Make sure you fully understand the other person (De-coding). • Summarise what has been discussed and make sure you agree next steps. • If the conversation veers off-track or the other person talks too much or too little, notice this and gently steer it back to the agreed objectives. |
| **REMEMBER** | Your attention is one of the most important gifts you can give other people! So practice showing it. | One of the most important ways to get the right outcome from your conversations is to be aware and in control of your own needs and emotions. So practice tuning into yourself. | If you improve only one Super-Skill make it this one, whether that be at work, with your partners, your friends or your neighbours. Remember we have two ears and one mouth – use them in that proportion. | This is perhaps the hardest Super-Skills because many of us associate speaking out with risk or causing arguments. But very few problems, at home or at work, are solved by not speaking about them – and we all feel better once we say what we really feel. | Great conversations don't just happen by accident. They require planning and the ability to be responsive during the conversation to ensure it stays on track. Your time is precious so use it wisely. |

# DFV ANALYSIS

Thinking like a designer can transform the way you innovate and develop solutions.

This approach, which is known as design thinking, brings together what is desirable from a human point of view with what is technologically feasible and economically viable.

It also allows people who aren't trained as designers to use creative tools to address a vast range of challenges.

Any idea taken forward should be desirable, feasible and viable.

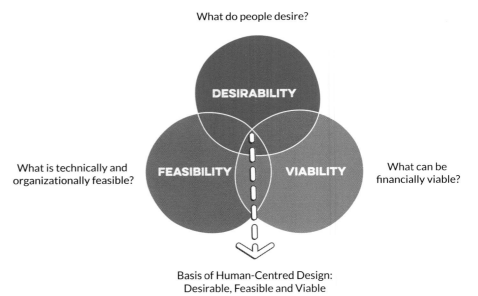

**HUMAN-CENTRED DESIGN**

What do people desire?

DESIRABILITY

What is technically and organizationally feasible?

FEASIBILITY

VIABILITY

What can be financially viable?

Basis of Human-Centred Design:
Desirable, Feasible and Viable

# "DESIGN THINKING IS A HUMAN-CENTERED APPROACH TO INNOVATION THAT DRAWS FROM THE DESIGNER'S TOOLKIT TO INTEGRATE THE NEEDS OF PEOPLE, THE POSSIBILITIES OF TECHNOLOGY, AND THE REQUIREMENTS FOR BUSINESS SUCCESS."

TIM BROWN
EXECUTIVE CHAIR OF IDEO

# 5 QUESTIONS

When making decisions it can be useful to step back and ask a series of top-level questions.

**Here they are:**
1. Is what we are about to do desirable, feasible and viable? It adds value to our customers, we have the resources to do it now, and the likely benefits outweigh the cost.
2. Does it make us more money?
3. Does it save us money or make money go out slower?
4. Does it make us compliant?
5. Is it fun?

Debating the questions will help your decision making.

# EASE IMPACT GRID

**What is it?**
A tool for prioritising action.

**How do I use it?**
Sheets of paper and some pens –
depending on where this is being
completed, in a team or group situation,
it is often best to use flip chart paper.

Start by summarising possible projects/
tasks/ideas and then number them.

Populate the grid based on ease of
doing and impact of doing.

Take top ideas that are easiest to do and
will have most impact.

Create plans for other ideas as
appropriate.

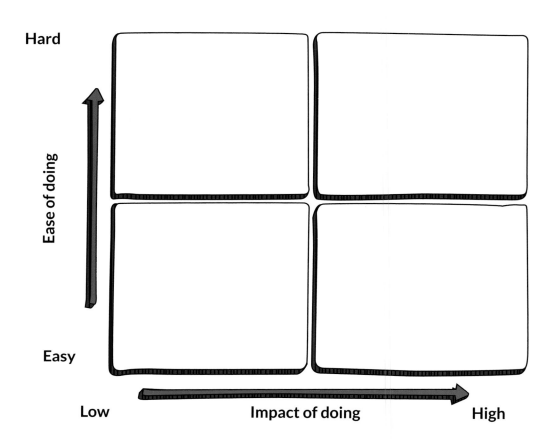

# WORLD CAFÉ

Using the ideas of others is really important to make effective decisions. We always say that inclusion = commitment. You want to use all the intellectual capital available.

World Café methodology is a simple, effective, and flexible format for hosting large group dialogue.

World Café can be modified to meet a wide variety of needs. Specifics of context, numbers, purpose, location, and other circumstances are factored into each event's unique invitation, design, and question choice, but the following five components comprise the basic model:

**Setting:** Create a "special" environment, most often modelled after a café, i.e. small round tables covered with a paper tablecloth, coloured pens, a vase of flowers, and optional "talking stick" item. There should be four chairs at each table.

**Welcome and Introduction:** The host begins with a warm welcome and an introduction to the World Café process, setting the context, sharing the café etiquette, and putting participants at ease.

**Small Group Rounds:** The process begins with the first of three or more rounds (length of time chosen by facilitator) of conversation for the small group seated around a table. At the end of the round, each member of the group moves to the next table. They may or may not choose to leave one person as the "table host" for the next round, who welcomes the next group and briefly fills them in on what happened in the previous round.

**Questions:** Each round is prefaced with a question designed for the specific context and desired purpose of the session. The same questions can be used for more than one round, or they can be built upon each other to focus the conversation or guide its direction.

**Harvest:** After the small groups (and/or in between rounds, as desired) individuals are invited to share insights or other results from their conversations with the rest of the large group. These results are reflected visually in a variety of ways.

Focus on what matters

Notice patterns. Connect ideas

SLOW DOWN

Slow Down So you have time to think and reflect

doodle

Play.. Draw..Doodle

Have fun!

Listen to learn

Contribute your thinking

Speak with your heart and mind

Facilitate yourself with others

# SO WHAT?

**List all the key learning insights you have gained from reading the book here.
What are they and why are they important to you?**

# NOW WHAT?

**List the key actions you are going to take.**
**Now pick no more than 3 actions to start with.**
**Make sure that the 3 you pick will have the most impact and are the easiest to do for you.**
**You can do the harder ones later!**

# WHAT NEXT?

Jenny and I hope you enjoyed wabisugi and have gained valuable insights into developing your new resilient life.

As they say, the key is to connect with the learning and apply it to your ways of working.

Turning what you've learned into new habits, routines, and rituals is the key to your success.

We wish you well on your journey and would love to hear how the book has helped you.

If you want to take your learning to the next level, we have an online course based on the book.

Take a look at **www.wabisugi.com** for details.

Every success

**Jenny and Graham**

**For further information on developing yourself and your team, visit:**

**thesuccessfactory.co.uk**

**grahamwilson.com**